SPONTANEOUS OPTIMISM™

Proven Strategies for Health, Prosperity & Happiness

by

Dr. Michael W. Mercer
&
Dr. Maryann V. Troiani

CASTLEGATE PUBLISHERS, INC.
830 West Main Street, Suite 107
Lake Zurich, Illinois, U.S.A. 60047
Phone = (847) 382-6420

Library of Congress Cataloging-in-Publication Data
Mercer, Michael W. 1950
Troiani, Maryann V. 1958
    Spontaneous Optimism
    Michael W. Mercer & Maryann V. Troiani
    ISBN 0-938901-09-5 :
    1. Self-help. 2. Self-improvement
    3. Psychology. I. Title.
    Library of Congress Catalog Card Number:
    97-075101
    158.1 - dc20
    Printing number
    10 9 8 7 6 5 4 3 2 1
    Printed in the United States of America.

TRADEMARKS:

    Spontaneous Optimism™ and *Positive Mind Conditioning*™ are trademarks of Castlegate Publishers, Inc. All rights reserved.

    Hire the Best--& Avoid the Rest™ and *Turning Your Human Resources Department into a Profit Center*™ are trademarks of The Mercer Group, Inc. All rights reserved.

    Behavior Forecaster™ and *Abilities Forecaster*™ are trademarks of Mercer Systems, Inc. All rights reserved.

    *Intensive Coaching*ᔆᴹ is a Service Mark of The Mercer Group, Inc. All rights reserved.

NOTE: This book aims to provide useful information. It is printed with the understanding that the publisher and the authors are not engaged in rendering professional service, counseling, therapy or medical help, through the contents of this book. If professional service is sought by a reader, such as counseling or psychotherapy or medical advice or other help, then the reader should seek the services of a competent professional.

Dedicated to

Idelle Pickard
the world's most optimistic aunt

&

J.S. Martindale, Ph.D.
an optimistic mentor

Contents

Preface

We felt compelled to write this book for both professional and personal reasons. In terms of *professional reasons*, we designed our book to prove vastly different — and superior — in three key ways from other books you may see on optimism-related topics:

1. Research

We cite research that *proves* what works and what does not work in a person's quest to become more optimistic. In sharp contrast, almost all other books on optimism-related topics cite only the author's opinions with few, if any, facts to *prove* they really may help you.

2. Professional Expertise

As psychologists with doctoral degrees, we have *over 30 years* combined experience using methods recommended in this book to help thousands of people. Maryann, a clinical or mental health psychologist, has used our methods to help clients vastly improve their lives. Michael, an industrial or business psychologist, has used our methods to help thousands of managers and professionals enhance their careers, productivity, and personal lives.

Jointly, we developed a unique Intensive Coaching^{SM} method that helps clients quicker (in only 3 - 6 hours, usually) and more profoundly than typical counseling procedures.

Also, we deliver over 100 speeches and workshops annually. Our presentations help groups of people exceed their own expectations.

As such, our book reveals to you special techniques we use. These methods have equipped large numbers of people to boost their optimism and success in both their personal and work lives. Now, you can benefit, too, from our extensive professional expertise.

3. We Help People Achieve Their Wildest Dreams

Everyone desires to feel enthusiastic and inspired to create an absolutely fabulous life. But, how do you start — and how do you actually do that? Our book shows you how. We distilled pragmatic tips from our speeches, workshops and Intensive Coaching^{SM} sessions into easy-to-use methods. You will create an exciting vision for your life, plus learn to transform your vision into reality. This is the key to changing your life from ordinary to extraordinary.

In addition to professional reasons we wrote this book, we also wrote it for important *personal reasons* that can help you.

1. We Use These Methods

We have, as mentioned earlier, over 30 years combined professional experience using our optimism methods with clients. This has provided us with a "laboratory" in which we discover first-hand what works and what does not work. We, of course, also "experiment" on ourselves to verify the usefulness of each method.

In our own search to achieve health, prosperity and happiness, we found the methods we show you work extremely well. Perhaps you will think us immodest for saying this, but we consider ourselves living proof that our methods really work.

Through our book, you will learn our "secrets." This is ultra-important for you. Why? Because you probably prefer to learn from authors who are living examples of what they write about.

2. Our Life Together

People we meet continually comment that we appear happy together. We consider this both a compliment and a fact. Being happy together seems increasingly rare for couples nowadays. We use our optimism methods to delightfully enhance our relationship. You, too, can benefit from putting our optimism techniques into action with the special people in your life.

Now, you have an opportunity to create an optimistic life. As we show you in our book, this can lead you to a life of increasing health, prosperity, and happiness.

We hope you enjoy the journey. We know you will cherish the results.

Positively,

Michael W. Mercer, Ph.D. & Maryann V. Troiani, Psy.D.

Acknowledgments

We greatly appreciate our families' love and the many things we learned from them: Our parents (Rhea, Philip, Josephine, and Edward), aunt (Idelle), brothers and sisters (Meridith, Joe, Dan, Jeffrey, and Eddie), nephews and nieces (Mike, Kim, Ed, Jill, and Joey).

Our friends have been wonderful cheerleaders. They include Dr. Rosemary Ciullo, Robert Cormack, Dr. Bruno Cortis, Barbara Jennifer Dahl, Dr. Abbey Graves, Lynn Greenstein, Linaya Hahn, David Hasmonek, Robert Hoffman, Dale Kerkman, Gisela M. Kubli, Ralf T. Kubli, Pamela Nelson, Heather Victoria Sterling, Dr. Paulette Trumm, Dr. Willa Wertheimer-Sexton, Sandra Zeidler.

We thank our many workshop participants and people who have attended our speeches. Through their questions and comments, we improved our ability to convey material in this book in a readily useful, easy-to-understand manner.

1

Introduction:

Why We Wrote This Book

Our book focuses on the the psychology of optimism.

We chose to become psycholgists because we enjoy feeling optimistic. We define optimism to include

- ◆ possessing a clear vision and dream of an exciting and fulfilling life
- ◆ pursuing goals that lead to achieving your vision for a wonderful future
- ◆ having a confident, positive, "can-do" attitude
- ◆ being in-control of personal and professional endeavors
- ◆ taking high levels of self-responsibility
- ◆ being out-going
- ◆ living a prosperous life

Before we started our doctoral training to become psychologists, we informally helped our friends and acquaintances overcome problems and enjoy life. This felt so exciting and fulfilling that we decided to enter psychology to help even more people.

However, while earning our doctoral degrees, we encountered many obstacles.

For instance, education to become psychologists tried to pollute our minds. Courses focused on illness, ill-thinking, and forever condemning people to mental illness "labels." In fact, when we did not label our clients as "alcoholic," "addict," "co-dependent," "borderline," or other psychobabble, we often became the brunt of ridicule. We even were considered odd by our professors and colleagues who felt enamored with putting sickness labels on others' behaviors.

Why don't we like to label people? Because a mental illness label gives people an excuse not to be fully responsible for their lives. For example, some people may claim, "I can't work, because I'm an addict!"

Mental illness labels give people excuses for acting dysfunctional. Labels also let people stay stuck in the dysfunction they personally chose. Professors taught us that people are controlled by their illnesses and are prisoners of their pasts. But, we both always knew deep in our hearts that optimistic people take self-responsibility and control of their lives, emotions, thoughts, and health.

In fact, we even were taught to exert all our budding therapeutic efforts to keep patients or clients in psychotherapy for the longest time possible. This approach flew in the face of our personal experiences showing people quickly can make startling insights and miraculous improvements.

Then, after completing our doctoral degrees, the reality of the practice of mental health professionals hit us between the eyes. We worked in mental health clinics, hospitals, and private practices. In those settings, we faced the perverted fact that mental health treatment often is <u>not</u> based on what specific techniques may really help the troubled individual.

Instead, we saw that much mental health treatment was determined by two factors that have a questionable connection to actually helping the patient:

1. The more money a patient could spend on treatment, the more therapy the person got — even if the therapy was not needed or helpful. This boiled down to rip-offs of insurance and patients' savings.

2. Treatment method often is techniques the therapist enjoys doing, regardless of whether or not the techniques help the patient. For example, psychiatric M.D.s love to prescribe drugs, even if a "talking cure" may help more. Non-M.D. mental health practitioners would use "talking cures" they most enjoyed using. For instance, some therapists would use psychoanalytic therapy on a patient who would have benefitted much more from simple, quick behavior modification.

These problems in the mental health *business* may best be illustrated by the fact that if you divide the word psychotherapist in a certain way, you get the word psycho-the-rap-ist. Specifically, sometimes patients are figuratively "raped" in terms of

- ◆ spending excessive amounts of money for treatment
- ◆ receiving treatment that may not be the best method for overcoming their troubles
- ◆ feeling upset or unhappy longer than necessary

Here are two examples to illuminate how trained mental health professionals may not know how to help you achieve mental health.

First, Michael served on an examining committee to give verbal exams to students graduating from a doctoral program in mental health. All the students could pontificate on every conceivable mental illness, such as neurosis, psychosis, schizophrenia, psychosomatic complaints, and so on *ad nauseum.*

However, when Michael asked them to define what "mental *health*" is,

- ◆ all the students appeared flabergasted and totally surprised by the question!
- ◆ none of the students could adequately answer!!
- ◆ some of them even remarked that defining mental *health* was not taught by any of their esteemed professors in four years of graduate school!!!
- ◆ all the students received very low scores on their explanations of what mental *health* is!!!!

Second, mental health professionals seem to be only minimally interested in people become more optimistic. For example, a review of articles cited in *Psychological Abstracts* over 17 years revealed a startling fact. During that lengthy period, there appeared about

- ◆ 60,000 articles on negative moods, such as depression, nervousness, and anger
- ◆ 2,400 studies about positive moods, for example, optimism and achieving satisfaction in life

This illustrates that mental health professors, researchers and even graduate students find it immensely more profitable and interesting to dwell on how you may fall on your face, rather than how you can pick yourself up.

Blazing A New Trail for Your Mental Health

As a result, we decided to blaze a new trail. We discovered we could vastly increase psychology's ability to improve people's lives. The techniques we present in our book are those we personally use all the time in our lives. Plus, our unique, specially developed, brief Intensive Coaching^{SM}

sessions with hundreds of clients show our methods are remarkably effective. In addition, we cite many research studies on techniques we suggest to illustrate their effectiveness.

Underlying our approach are key principles. By accepting these principles, you lay the groundwork to find our techniques immediately effective. Our principles are the foundation of building new health for your head.

Principle 1: Change Won't Take Forever

Unfortunately, improving yourself fairly quickly used to be a rather mysterious art. Fortunately, we will show you methods to improve your life via simple, ready-to-use methods. And you can start today and see results fast. In fact, many techniques you learn in this book will take you only 60 seconds to put into action!

Principle 2: Don't Stay Stuck In Your Past

Improving your life does not need to involve "anal-yzing" what you want to change. Avoid wasting your time wallowing in the question, "Why am I this way?" Instead, in this book you learn specific ways to improve your life. You obtain important personal improvement techniques so you can take action immediately and just do it!

*"It is one thing to learn about the past;
it is another to wallow in it."*

KENNETH AUCHINCLOSS

Principle 3: Not Improving Your Life Can Be a Living Nightmare

Most people dread changing as much as they dread a plague. However, *not* changing your habits that harm you is like allowing a disease to creep into your psyche and gnaw a hole in your sense of well-being. Despite the emotional cancer people inflict on themselves, many people put off doing what they know deep in their hearts could brighten their existence.

As the proverb goes:

If you do what you've always done,
then you'll just get what you've always gotten.

Principle 4: Role Models Make It Easy for You

The easiest, quickest and most successful way to improve yourself is to
- ◆ find a "role model" who effectively does what you want to do
- ◆ do what your "role model" does

It really is that simple. You learn how to succeed from people who are successful. Do not expect to learn nearly as much from people who are not successful in what you want to do.

For example, if you want to act more lively and outgoing, find someone who is lively and outgoing. Study your role model. For instance, what does she do to appear more lively and outgoing? How does the person walk, talk and carry herself? Then, copy or adapt your role model's behaviors and attitudes.

A key reason you may not have made desired improvements is because you never observed or studied *role models* and techniques used by successful people who

- ◆ improve their lives
- ◆ do it quickly and effectively
- ◆ have fun at the same time

Principle 5: Imagine You Are A Parachute

To improve your life very quickly, you simply need to think of yourself as follows:

Your mind is like a parachute:
It works better when it's open!

As you read our book, keep your mind open to new
- ◆ ideas
- ◆ ways to accomplish what you desire to do

Allow yourself to experiment with these new methods. If you do not want to use one technique we suggest, then just do not use it. Simply find another one you feel comfortable using. The main point is that you will have at your fingertips many ways to improve yourself in the areas you decide you want to improve. It is like the fact that $2 + 2 = 3 + 1$. All you should care about is that you achieve your desired results.

"If not now — then when?"

HILLEL

Remember: You need to experiment with these techniques *over and over* until you
- ◆ get it right
- ◆ choose the methods that you feel best about using

Repeated practice makes these techniques become automatic habits and second nature to you.

"Our greatest glory is not in never falling, but in rising every time we fall."

CONFUCIOUS

Principle 6: Let Your Actions Precede Your Feelings

If you wait until you *emotionally feel* ready to make improvements, you might turn into dust before you take any *action*. Many people do not pursue their dreams or aspirations because they let fear, doubt or laziness get in their way.

Fortunately, psychological research has found that *actions can precede emotions.* For instance, many people fear (emotion) public speaking (action). A good way to overcome your fear is not to tremble or think too much about it. Instead, just take action — give a speech — and in doing so you eventually begin to feel more confident and less fearful about public speaking.

"Be the change you're trying to create."

MAHATMA GHANDI

So, now the question that looms large is, "How do I deal with the fear or unpleasant emotions that keep me from chasing my goals?" Answer: *Fake it until you make it.* Take action — almost any action that helps you improve yourself or achieve your goals, regardless of how you feel at the moment. Rivet your emotions on how proud you will feel when you achieve your goals. Avoid concentrating on how you might stumble as you climb the mountain.

In our research on successful people, those we interviewed mentioned that many times in their lives they "just jumped in the pool and figured out how to swim." They never admitted they did not know exactly what to do or felt scared.

*"Your first step **always** is to
take your first step."*

MARYANN V. TROIANI

Principle 7: Take Total Responsibility for Improving Your Life

Once upon a time . . . .

Remember the role that fairy tales played in your childhood. Characters in those tales got into all sorts of jams. Then, all of a sudden, Superman or Prince Charming or another figure with magical powers swoops in to rescue the main character from certain doom. What a relief!

Unfortunately, no such super-heroes or knights-in-shining-armor or other enchanting rescuers show up in real life. Instead, you must stumble or progress on your own. Of course, some people may help you. Some may give you wise advice. Others offer you hands-on assistance.

Most importantly, in the outcome, you achieve as little — or as much — as you want. Remember:

*"No one ever succeeded
through the dazzling brilliance
of their excuses."*

MICHAEL W. MERCER

We find people who are unsuccessful and avoid improving their lives excell at using *excuse-itis*. They can give you excuses or rationales for going nowhere. In sharp contrast, optimistic, successful people take total responsibility for their lives.

These principles form the foundation of our groundbreaking technique of Intensive Coaching^{SM} and our Positive Mind Conditioning™ methods. In the brief Intensive Coaching^{SM} sessions we conduct with individuals and couples, we apply these principles to help people quickly make fast and dramatic improvements. And now, with this book, you have our special techniques in your hands — and ready to use yourself.

2

Why Be Optimistic?

You, of course, picked up this book so you can learn how to boost your optimism. In brief, an optimistic person

- ◆ possesses a clear vision of an exciting, meaningful life
- ◆ works on goals to help progress toward his or her exciting vision
- ◆ has a confident, "Can-Do" attitude
- ◆ exerts much personal control over his or her life
- ◆ takes high levels of self-responsibility
- ◆ is outgoing
- ◆ lives a prosperous life

Importantly, many motivational books preached to you that you must display positive attitudes. However, they seldom proved to you that their techniques work. Fortunately, we provide to you our *over 30 years combined experience as psychologists* plus *research studies* that show you throughout this book that optimism

- ◆ positively affects many areas of your life
- ◆ is easy to learn

"Perpetual optimism is a force multiplier."

COLIN POWELL

How would you benefit from becoming more optimistic? Our research reveals three main benefits from being optimistic. Specifically, *being optimistic can help you become more healthy, prosperous, and happy.*

Reason #1: Optimism Helps Improve Your Health

Research shows optimistic people exhibit higher levels of mental and physical health than pessimistic people. Let's look at how.

Improve Your Mental Health

We believe a crucial ingredient of mental health is optimism.
    For example, in our psychological work with clients, we observe that optimistic people

- ◆ have high self-esteem
- ◆ feel in-control of their lives
- ◆ exhibit a "Can-Do" attitude
- ◆ act as cheerleaders for themselves and others

In sharp contrast, people who continually feel emotionally upset tend to be pessimistic or lacking in optimism. That explains why they go through life with uncomfortable feelings gushing though their brains.

Supporting our belief and psychological observations that optimism is a key factor in mental health is a report in *The Harvard Mental Health Letter*.[1] It states that psychology professors David Myers, Ph.D., and Edward Diener, Ph.D., found four traits that distinguish happy people. These four traits are

- ◆ high self-esteem
- ◆ feeling in control of their lives
- ◆ being optimistic
- ◆ acting outgoing

Drs. Myers and Diener report that surveys suggest that positive thinking is instrumental to happiness. As such, our belief and argument that optimism improves your mental health is supported by research.

A leading researcher on optimism is Martin Seligman, Ph.D., professor of psychology at the University of Pennsylvania. In summarizing his findings on pessimism — the opposite of optimism — Dr. Seligman found that pessimism leads to

- ◆ depression
- ◆ worry and tension
- ◆ hopelessness
- ◆ setbacks and frustration

"All happiness is in the mind."

ENGLISH PROVERB

Experiencing these reactions can create a downward spiral of despair and emotional turmoil. It is like a snowball rolling downhill, picking up more snow and velocity until it finally smacks into a tree at the bottom of the hill. Such may be the fate of someone who does not lift himself or herself out of pessimism and into optimism.

Improve Your Physical Health

Research comparing optimistic people with pessimistic people shows that people with high levels of optimism
- are healthier
- get well or heal faster than people who are pessimistic

On the other hand, pessimists tend to
- get sick more often
- take longer to get well or heal

In general, it appears that much physical health or illness is an external symbol of our internal optimism or pessimism. Optimism tends to reveal itself in physical wellness. In contrast, pessimism can rear its ugly head through disease, sickness, and even the common cold. In fact, studies have shown a significant relationship between negative feelings — such as anger, anxiety, stress, and depression — and headaches.[2, 3, 4]

Let's look at key research findings you should find eye-opening in your quest to boost your optimism and wellness. One of the first physicians to explore how moods impact health is O. Carlton Simonton, M.D., medical director of the Cancer Counseling and Research Center in Fort Worth, Texas. He co-authored the book *Getting Well Again*.[5] Dr. Simonton's research found

- ◆ the more a person feels emotionally upset or stressed, the more likely the person will become ill
- ◆ the longer a person feels emotionally upset, combined with pessimistic attitudes, the more susceptible the person is to major illnesses
- ◆ importantly, a person's emotional stress level is determined by the person's attitude toward possibly stressful life events; seemingly negative events are not stressful themselves; it is a person's perspective on the events make them emotionally stressful or not

Dr. Simonton's findings illustrate the importance of learning — and actually using — techniques to boost your optimism. Doing so can vastly improve your health, or at least leave you less susceptible to illness.

Studies by researcher S.N. Haynes and his colleagues support Dr. Simonton's earlier findings that stress, and specifically prolonged stress, can affect health. They exposed headache sufferers to a prolonged stressor and found that headaches occurred in 83% of their subjects.[6]

Along the same lines as Dr. Simonton, Deepak Chopra, M.D., author of *Quantum Healing* and other groundbreaking books, asserts that a person's mood actually changes his or her physiology.[7, 8] For instance, a person feeling happy has a healthier physiology and immune system than when he or she feels depressed.

"Happiness is the most powerful of tonics."

HERBERT SPENCER

Dr. Chopra's assertion has been proven in research. For example, a report in *The Harvard Mental Health Letter* states that several studies found severely depressed patients have impaired immune systems.[9] Also, a joint University of Pennsylvania and Dartmouth medical school research project discovered that optimistic Harvard graduates developed diseases less often than their pessimistic Harvard classmates.[10] In addition, multiple studies illustrate that stress and anxiety alter components of cellular immunity.[11, 12]

Cardiologist Bruno Cortis, M.D., has treated and studied "exceptional heart patients." These patients are people who recover from typically life-threatening heart conditions. Many go on to live healthier, more fulfilling and happier lives than they did before their severe heart problems.

How do they perform such miracles on themselves? Dr. Cortis reports in his insightful book *Heart & Soul* that "exceptional heart patients... respond to their condition with optimism and hope."[13]

A merry heart doeth good like medicine.

English Proverb

A large-scale 29-year research study led by Susan Everson of the California Department of Health[14] found depressed people, compared to non-depressed people, proved
- ◆ 50 percent more likely to suffer strokes
- ◆ 50 percent more likely to die from their strokes

Another interesting study done at South Florida University, by professor and immune system expert Nicholas Hall, found stressed people are more likely than their less stressed counterparts to

◆ catch a cold
◆ have a cold for a long time

And a research project done by England's Medical Research Council's Common Cold Unit found that high-stress people, when exposed to a virus, were two times as likely to get sick than low-stress people.[15]

These research studies show the mind plays a huge role in a person's health. And the key mental talent used by healthy people is optimism. This includes self-confidence, taking total responsibility for one's life, and a "Can-Do" attitude.

This was demonstrated in pioneering biofeedback studies by Maryann and psychologist J.S. Martindale, Ph.D., professor at Northeastern Illinois University.[16, 17] Biofeedback is a method in which people learn how to use their brains to control and, thus, improve their physical health.

For example, one biofeedback subject had a tumor. Using biofeedback techniques, the woman learned to

◆ sharply focus her thoughts
◆ use visualization techniques
◆ productively manage her stress

Using these methods, the woman vividly imagined — or visualized — her tumor dissolving like a tablet dropped in water.

Lo and behold, when the woman later saw her physician, she discovered her tumor disappeared! She actually used her mind to heal herself.

Finally, your optimism can even help you live longer. Professor David P. Phillips of the University of California in

San Diego studied this phenomenon. He found extremely sick people actually can keep themselves from dying until after a special event occurs in their lives.[18] For example, Maryann's grandfather was lying on his deathbed. No one expected him to live much longer. However, he kept saying he wanted to see the birth of his first granddaughter. He made a decision to live longer. He hung on to his life, and died shortly after his first granddaughter, Maryann, was born. This example illustrates the power of your attitudes. You actually can decide to live longer or die. These powerful decisions give optimistic people tremendous control over their longevity and health.

Reason #2: Optimism Links To Financial Prosperity

Thomas J. Stanley, Ph.D., and William D. Danko, Ph.D., probably are the world's foremost researchers of affluent people. In their fascinating and highly useful book, *The Millionaire Next Door*, they carefully detail the tactics and lifestyles of *self-made* millionaires.[19] These are not trust-fund recipients, people handed vast sums of money, or individuals who achieved just one windfall. Most do not make huge amounts of money each year. Instead, these are *self-made* millionaires who responsibly work hard, save money, invest wisely, and lead frugal lifestyles.

Throughout their book, Drs. Stanley and Danko compare two types of people:

◆ PAWs:
   Prodigious Accumulators of Wealth who have become self-made millionaires
◆ UAWs:
   Under Accumulators of Wealth; UAWs earn just as much as PAWs per year, but they do not become millionaires

Importantly, PAWs take actions to accumulate wealth. But, UAWs spend lots of energy and time worrying, rather than taking active steps to solve their worries.

Drs. Stanley and Danko compared a typical PAW with a typical UAW on a list of 31 possible topics to worry about. Intriguingly, the

+ PAW listed seven worries, six of moderate concern and one of high concern
+ UAW listed 19 worries, 15 of moderate concern and four of high concern

This dramatically illustrates that people who keep plugging away to accumulate wealth — become self-made millionaires — seem more likely to be optimistic people. PAWs appear to be people who proceed with a planned out, "Can-Do," confident approach to achieving financial security. As such, they give themselves less to worry about than UAWs.

In sharp contrast, UAWs spend more time fretting than their more affluent PAW counterparts. Apparently, UAWs waste their time worrying and overspending rather than creating a secure financial future.

Another well-researched report about prosperous people appeared in *Worth* magazine.[20] *Worth* and the Roper Starch polling organization did a survey of the top one percent of the U.S. population, in terms of net worth. These 2.6 million affluent people are worth a median of $2.34 million.

When asked for the key to getting ahead, the most frequent response (82%) was that *tremendous persistence* was extremely important. Great persistence readily translates into what we describe as optimists' characteristic confidence, tenacity, and "Can-Do" attitude — combined with lots of work. That is, the top 1-percenters live and breathe — and financially benefit from — optimism.

You, too, can join the top 1-percenters. After all, over a recent 15 year period, about 30 percent of people in the lowest fifth of the economic ladder raised themselves up into

the highest fifth. Apparently, optimism has its financial rewards. Later in this book, you can read an entire chapter devoted to helping you greatly improve your finances and increase your net worth — including many ideas on how you
can become a millionaire.

Reason #3: Optimistic People Achieve More Career Success

Michael consistently finds that people who achieve career
success are optimistic. He developed two tests used by many
companies to predict which applicants may turn out to be
productive, dependable employees. One of these is the *Behavior Forecaster*™ test.[21, 22] This test predicts — or forecasts
— 14 work-related behaviors, including optimism.

To customize the *Behavior Forecaster*™ testing for a company, Michael does a "benchmarking" study. First, the company decides which job it wants to test candidates for. Second, *successful* employees in that job are tested using the *Behavior Forecaster*™ test and sometimes also the *Abilities
Forecaster*™ tests.* Unsuccessful employees in the same job
may be tested, too. Third, then it is easy to pinpoint which
scores typically are gotten by the successful and unsuccessful employees. Fourth, the company has applicants fill-out
the *Behavior Forecaster*™ test. The company then can show
preference for applicants who score similar to its successful
employees in the job.

You can take the *Behavior Forecaster*™ and *Abilities Forecaster*™ tests yourself. On
the *Behavior Forecaster*™, you will receive your scores on 14 interpersonal skills,
personality traits (including optimism), and work motivations. From the *Abiltities
Forecaster*™, you will receive your scores on five mental abilities. To try out the
tests, simply use the "Materials You Can Order" section at the back of this book.
If you want to read more about how to hire successful employees, you can read
Michael's book, *Hire the Best — & Avoid the Rest*™. Again, you can use the "Materials You Can Order" section in the back of this book.

Here is an astounding finding: Every time Michael does a benchmarking study on successful employees, the successful employees always score average to high on the Optimism scale. However, the unsuccessful employees in the same jobs in the same companies tend to get more moderate or even low scores on the Optimism scale of the *Behavior Forecaster*™ test.

This is clear, repeated proof that people who are successful in their careers tend to be optimistic people. In contrast, their less successful colleagues are not nearly as optimistic. This dramatically illustrates the importance of optimism for your career success.

"Success seems to be connected with action.
Successful people keep moving.
They make mistakes, but they don't quit."

CONRAD HILTON

Summary

Below you will find a checklist summarizing the points you read in this chapter. *Suggestion:* On each line, *circle* the word or phrase that best describes you. This helps you pinpoint how you use your optimism — or pessimism — in terms of your health, wealth, and career success.

Pessimism Promotes...	**Optimism Promotes...**
Depression	Happiness
Anxiety	Confidence
Letting obstacles to stand in your way	Rising above obstacles
Dwelling on problems	Dwelling on opportunities
Career problems	Career success
Much worrying	Little worrying
Lousy feelings	Good feelings
Illness	Health
Expecting things to go wrong	Expecting to figure out how to succeed
Hopelessness	Hopefulness
Financial problems	Prosperity

3

You Don't Need 2 Years Of Psychotherapy To Feel Optimistic:

You Just Need To Use These 60-Second Tips

In this chapter, you will learn five key techniques to feel spontaneously optimistic. You can benefit from these in a few ways. First, if you did nothing else except use these five tips, you definitely should feel noticeably more upbeat.

Second, you will find it vastly easier to make improvements in your life — as we show you in other chapters — when you feel optimistic. After all, when you are in a positive state of mind you are more

- ◆ open to helpful ideas
- ◆ likely to experiment with new ways to improve your life

So, we highly recommend you use the five techniques from this chapter each time you want to delve into any other methods to improve your health, prosperity, and happiness.

Third, in our Intensive Coaching^{SM} sessions with hundreds of clients, we always use these five techniques. It never ceases to amaze us how these simple tactics help form the basic foundation from which our clients vastly improve their lives.

Technique #1: Use Straight Posture

Depressed people slouch. Their shoulders roll forward and their heads hang down.

Optimistic people tend to use straight posture. They keep their heads up, shoulders back, and chests out.

Most clients who come to us for Intensive Coaching[SM] sessions walk into the office and then slouch. We immediately tell them to straighten up. In fact, we often use the following phrase:

*"Before you can straighten out your head,
you first need to straighten up your body."*

MICHAEL W. MERCER & MARYANN V. TROIANI

Our recommendation to you is to continually check your body posture. Notice that when you slouch, your mood takes somewhat of a dive. When you notice that, immediately straighten up. That is your first step to boost your mood.

Technique #2: Use Cheerful Voice Tone

Here is an incredibly useful but seldom publicized psychological insight: A person *feels* whatever emotion he or she is *acting* out at that moment.

"The greatest discovery of my generation is that human beings can alter their lives by altering their attitudes of mind."

WILLIAM JAMES

So, when you want to feel happy, act happy. If you want to feel romantic, act romantic. If you want to feel depressed (as some people do!), then act depressed.

A report in *The Harvard Mental Health Letter* reviewed research that support this psychological insight.[1] Psychology professors David Myers, Ph.D., and Edward Diener, Ph.D., reveal that it appears possible to feel happier by acting-out the traits of happy people. Four key traits of happy people are

- high self-esteem
- feelings in control of one's life
- being optimistic
- acting out-going

For instance, in experiments it was found that people who pretend they have high self-esteem actually begin to feel better about themselves. Also, research subjects who were told to smile as part of an experiment actually felt happier.

We find the best way to instantly feel optimistic is to use a cheerful tone of voice.

*"If you want a quality, act as if you already
had it. Try the 'as if' technique."*

WILLIAM JAMES

Think about it: When you speak in a serious tone of voice,
you feel serious. Depressed people use a low, slow, "down"
tone of voice. An optimistic person injects cheerfulness into
his or her voice.

For example, a man came to us for an Intensive
Coaching^{SM} session to figure out his career goals and get
motivated. He walked into our office in a slouched posture,
and spoke in a downright depressed-sounding voice. Then,
he wondered aloud why he felt down and could not find
any direction in his life. We immediately had him correct his
posture and voice tone to a more optimistic style. Plus, we
also had him use the next technique...

Technique #3: Use Upbeat Words

Words you use affect your emotions and attitudes. We dramatically learned this during a conversation with an industrial psychologist who had tested many candidates for executive jobs. One day, he said,

> *I've tested some of the most successful executives in the
> U.S. and Canada, so I've learned many fascinating things
> about highly successful people. And one of the most fasci-
> nating things I have learned is that highly successful
> people never say they feel **nervous**. Instead, sometimes
> they say they feel **concerned**.*

His story revealed a tremendous insight. Highly successful people avoid using negative words, like *nervous*. Instead, they use more neutral or positive words, like *concerned*. By just changing your words from negative to neutral or positive, you emotionally change how you feel.

"A man is what he thinks about all day long."

RALPH WALDO EMERSON

In general, you could use these three types of words:
+ Positive words
0 Neutral words
- Negative words

For example, we do not know anyone who feels thrilled about making a *change*. After all, *change* can be negative. However, people feel excited about making *improvements*. So, instead of saying, "I'm going to make a change," we recommend you say, "I'm going to make an improvement." By doing that, you take the upsetting, negative edge off of *change* by referring to it as an *improvement* which you certainly would look forward to.

Or, you could say, "I have a *problem*." That feels somewhat upsetting to say. Instead, you will find it a relief to say, "Now, I have an *opportunity* to do this better." If you are like most people, you feel vastly more enthused about an *opportunity* than a *problem*.

*If you wish to know the mind of a man,
listen to his words.*

CHINESE PROVERB

Homework: In the left column of the following table, list upsetting words you use. Then, in the right column, list neutral or positive words you can substitute. We include a few examples to help you get started.

Upsetting Word	Upbeat Word
Nervous	Concerned
Problem	Opportunity
Change	Improvement
Overwhelmed	Challenged
Tired	Recharging
Frustrated	Redirecting
Confused	Discovering
_____	_____
_____	_____
_____	_____

Technique #4: Exude Upbeat Attitudes

Here is the key — the ultimate — the most important bit of

information for you to feel optimistic:

- ◆ Pessimistic, depressed people focus on *complaining.*
- ◆ Optimistic, happy people focus on *solving.*

"An optimist may see a light where there is none, but why must the pessimist always run to blow it out?"

MICHEL DE SAINT-PIERRE

It really is that simple. People who come to us for Intensive Coaching^SM sessions usually walk into our office complaining, moaning, and groaning (while slouching, sounding down, and using negative words).

Within two minutes, we usually say something like, "We know that situation is difficult for you. What's your possible *solution*?"

They must dramatically redirect their energy and focus when they *dwell on solving, rather than complaining.* Suddenly, tough problems become solvable challenges.

You can do the same. The next time you find yourself complaining, stop yourself in your tracks. Say to yourself, "What's my possible solution?" Doing this puts you on the road to Spontaneous Optimism™.

For example, you could focus on *complaining.* Or you could focus on *solutions.*

You could focus on *drawbacks.* Or you could focus on *opportunities.*

You could feel *tense.* Or you could feel *confident* about

your ability to figure out what you will do.

Homework: In the following table, in the left column, list some of your upsetting attitudes that you allowed to drag you down. Then, in the right column, list upbeat attitudes you plan to replace them with.

Upsetting Attitude	Upbeat Attitude
Complaining	Solving
Focus on drawbacks	Focus on opportunities
Tense	Confident
_____	_____
_____	_____
_____	_____

Technique #5: Be A Role Model

Let us tell you a story about someone we know. Her name is Victoria.

Throughout her life, people continually called Victoria names. As a baby, Victoria fell down a basement flight of stairs and was injured. Physicians told Victoria's parents she was slightly "damaged."

In grammar school, Victoria had difficulty with academics. Victoria's teachers called her parents, and told them she was "slow." The teachers even put Victoria in the slow learning group. Victoria felt humiliated.

In high school, Victoria still had difficulty with academics. She began to hang around with troublemakers. Her teachers called her parents, and said Victoria was a "delinquent."

In her senior year of high school, Victoria met a teacher who helped her become interested and excited about learning. This teacher was very supportive. Victoria suddenly wanted to go to college. In a meeting with her guidance counselor, the counselor exclaimed, "No one in their right mind would consider you college material!" Victoria burst into tears.

To this day, quite a few years later, people still call Victoria names. Today, they continually call her "Doctor" — Dr. Maryann *Victoria* Troiani — one of this book's authors.

How did Maryann overcome such challenges? Her key is that even with many potential obstacles, she remained an optimistic person.

Let her story be a role model for you to learn how to overcome obstacles. Then, as you succeed, you can serve as a role model of an optimistic person. As you show others how you succeed using an optimistic, "Can-Do" approach, you simultaneously help yourself as you help others.

It takes little effort to drag your feet in life and be a plague to yourself and those around you.

But, a truly exceptional person serves as a role model for those around him or her. In fact, later is this book, you can benefit from an entire chapter on how to be a role model who helps others become more optimistic.

Homework: List a few people for whom you could serve as a role model of an optimistic, "Can-Do" human being. These may be family members, friends, co-workers, and employees. Also, write one action you can frequently do in front of them so they will see you in action as an optimistic person.

**Person Who Could Consider
You A Role Model**   **Action You Can Take**

_____   _____

_____   _____

_____   _____

4

De-tox Your Mind:

Get Rid of Your Agony Anchors that Hold You Back

Introduction to Housecleaning Your Head

Water cannot flow though a pipe if the pipe is clogged.

Similarly, your personal stream of positive emotions cannot possibly flow through you — and improve your life — unless you remove the mental "clogs" stopping up your optimistic
- emotions
- thoughts

Most people need to houseclean their minds of the clogs, cobwebs, dirt and mold that take up valuable space. Fortunately, you do not need to waste your valuable time and money lying on a shrink's couch to do this. Instead, to help you unclog your mind today, we will show you
- key to your optimism
- ways to discard your Agony Anchors that hold you back
- how to clear your mind of your negative feelings and thoughts
- Positive Mind Conditioning™

Key To Being Optimistic

You could spend the next 365 days studying all the research, philosophy and tactics used to succeed in life. When you finish your in-depth study, you then can sit back and ponder this question: "So, what is the common thread that runs through most happiness and life successes?"

The answer is that optimistic people and people who succeed in life are incredibly *self-responsible.*

"It's very simple:
The more responsiblity you take for everything
you do and feel, the happier and more
successful you will be.
The less responsiblity you take for your life, the
more likely you will feel pessimistic, worried,
and perhaps even out-of-control.
It really is that simple!"

MICHAEL W. MERCER & MARYANN V. TROIANI

Unhappy, unsuccessful people avoid taking full responsibility for their lives, actions, thoughts, and feelings.

How do they pull off this unenviable feat? They resort to two very irresponsible behaviors. They

♦ want, demand, expect and manipulate others to take care of them; they spend much brainpower, energy and time searching for give-aways

♦ blame all sorts of people and situations for their predicaments

We call this *irresponsible-itis*. It is a bad habit that leads to terrible disease.

*"Don't go around saying
the world owes you a living; the world owes
you nothing; it was here first."*

MARK TWAIN

Get Rid of Agony Anchors that Hold You Back

Imagine a ship trying to sail. But, the captain does not bother to pull up its anchor. That holds the ship back. It cannot go anywhere.

You are the "captain" in your own life. It is hard — if not impossible — to get anywhere in your life if you do not cut your anchors loose.

Most people's anchors are what we call *"Agony Anchors."*

These emotional anchors are like continually listening to harsh recordings that hurt your head. But, many people habitually use agony anchors to make sure they do not improve their lives. They use three main types of Agony Anchors to keep from moving toward what they most want in life:

◆ Blame
◆ Negative feelings and thoughts
◆ Distractions

*"We need to recognize the tremendous power
which lies in all of us and which we cannot use
as long as we feel victimized."*

RUDOLF DREIKURS, M.D.

Agony Anchor #1: Blaming

People who fail in arenas of life often blame
- other people
- themselves

They blame other people for their difficulties. These can include parents, teachers, siblings, neighbors, friends, enemies, colleagues, and anyone else they can think of blaming for any affront. When these people bothered you, it probably was appropriate to cringe. However, at some point you need to stop ruminating about it and move on.

Another focus of blame is on yourself. You can chastise yourself for all sorts of possible faults. Perhaps you are too old, too young, too tall, too short, too skinny, too large, too educated, to uneducated, or manifest a million other defects. Again, at some point, people who lead optimistic lives cut loose these Agony Anchors and sail forward.

"How unhappy is he
who cannot forgive himself."

PUBLILIUS SYRUS

We developed three ways you can use right away to stop blaming others or yourself and take responsibility for your life successes.

First, you can write a letter to the person you blame for holding you back. You even can write a letter to yourself. Tell the person what he or she did to you that you find distasteful. Express how you feel. Let it all out!

Then, you can throw away the letter, burn it, or mail it to the person. Do whichever you feel most comfortable doing. Just make sure you do that, so you create a sense of finished business so you can move on. If you do mail the letter to the person who hurt you, do not expect a response that heals your mental wounds. That person may ignore your letter or overreact. For this reason, we generally recommend people not mail the letter. Instead, preferably tear it up or burn it.

Second, talk to the person who hurt you. Say, "You did something that left me feeling uncomfortable. Please let me tell you about it and how I felt." Most people will get defensive and try to refute your allegations. So, say to the person, "Please just let me say everything without you responding for a few minutes. I would really appreciate that."

Then, in a *calm* voice tell the person
- why you feel a need to tell this
- what he or she did that hurt you
- your reactions to that person's behavior

This is a cathartic experience.

*"To be wronged is nothing
unless you continue to remember it."*

CONFUCIUS

However, to really help you resolve your Agony Anchor of blame, use the third method. Specifically, use understanding in a special way. An enlightened method to dissolve blame is to understand and forgive. Perhaps you feel this would be difficult. Actually, we find many people resolve blame using our *"Getting Over Blame"* exercise.

To do this, you simply complete the *Getting Over Blame Form* shown here. On it, you list

- ◆ name of a *person* you blame for some of your current woes
- ◆ specific *actions* that person did that bothered you
- ◆ your *feelings* about those distasteful actions
- ◆ *reasons* why those lousy actions may have been the only or best way that person knew how to act, given their limited emotional state, brainpower, and interpersonal skills

Homework: Look at the example. Then, fill-out the *Getting Over Blame Form* for your own good.

Example of
Getting Over Blame Form

Name of Person I Blame: <u>Lee Doe</u>

Actions You Did That Hurt Me	Feelings I Had After You Did That	Reasons You Treated Me Lousy
1. Screamed	1. Horror	1. Childish
2. Drove away without me	2. Abandoned	2. Selfish
3. Lied to me	3. Anger	3. Desperate
4. Broke promise	4. Hurt	4. Inconsiderate, irresponsible

Now, I know your lousy actions were the best you could do at that time, given your limited emotional state, brainpower, and interpersonal skills.

Now, I forgive you for what you did.

Now, from this day onward, I take responsibility if I harbor these uncomfortable feelings (see middle column, above) in *any* part of my life.

_____   ___ / ___ / ___

My Signature   Date

Getting Over Blame Form

Name of Person I Blame: _____

Actions You Did That Hurt Me	Feelings I Had After You Did That	Reasons You Treated Me Lousy
1.	1.	1.
2.	2.	2.
3.	3.	3.
4.	4.	4.

Now, I know your lousy actions were the best you could do at that time, given your limited emotional state, brainpower, and interpersonal skills.

Now, I forgive you for what you did.

Now, from this day onward, I take responsibility if I harbor these uncomfortable feelings (see middle column, above) in *any* part of my life.

_____   ___ / ___ / ___

My Signature   Date

If you used our recommendations to overcome Agony Anchor #1: Blame, then *congratulations!!!!* You released your Agony Anchor #1.

Agony Anchor #2: Negative Feelings & Thoughts

From our years of counseling people, studying human behavior and research, we discovered that people experience
many negative feelings, especially

- ◆ Anger
- ◆ Bruised feelings
- ◆ Depression
- ◆ Guilt
- ◆ Low self-confidence
- ◆ Worry

As you read this list of unpleasant emotions, you probably thought, "Yuck!! Those are lousy feelings!!!!"

But, we find many, many people actually take some comfort in experiencing anger, bruised feelings, depression, guilt,
low self-confidence, and worry.

Why? Because experiencing these emotions is

- ◆ familiar
- ◆ gives them never-ending excuses for not improving their lives

*"When I look back on my worries, I remember
the story of the old man who said on his
deathbed that he had a lot of trouble in his life
— most of which never happened."*

WINSTON CHURCHILL

For example, we did Intensive Coaching[SM] sessions with
a woman who was a freelance writer. Her mother, whom she
adored, also had done freelance writing for small, local newspapers and low-circulation magazines. Likewise, our client
spent years writing for small, local periodicals.

Our immensely talented client longed to write articles
for big, national magazines. However, she kept hesitating to
call the big magazines' editors to suggest article ideas or request writing assignments. She cooked up every possible excuse.

In our first Intensive Coaching[SM] session with her, we
quickly cut through her abundant list of creative excuses.

To help her, we asked her the *Magic Question* that cuts to
the core of negative feelings. The *Magic Question* is "What do
you get out of those lousy feelings?"

In our client's case, underlying all her excuses was her
guilt. She feared she might do better than her mother ever
did. That fear led her to worry that her success may make
her mother feel like a failure.

What a large parade of Agony Anchors! The following
diagram shows you her Agony Anchor line-up:

Desire to succeed	→	Guilt	→	Worry	→	Inaction	→	Low Self-Confidence	→	Bruised Feelings

This case example shows you how a person continuously
uses unhelpful Agony Anchors, because they
   ◆ are familiar
   ◆ gave her automatic excuses for not improving
      her life

> *"As a man thinketh in his heart, so is he."*
>
> KING SOLOMAN

How To Eject Your Agony Anchor #2: Negative Feelings & Thoughts

To help you, we highly recommend you complete this simple exercise *now:*

Step 1: From your last 48 hours, list all your
   A. Positive feelings
   B. Negative feelings (Agony Anchors)

Step 2: Next to each negative feeling, answer the *Magic Question,* "What am I getting out of having that lousy feeling?"

Step 3: Next to each negative feeling, answer these .two questions —
   A. How have I hurt myself by having this negative feeling?
   B. How will I hurt myself if I continue to use this negative feeling for another two years? Imagine this now.

Please note that people we coach often answer the *Magic Question* (see Step 2) by saying, "I don't know." When we hear that, we always respond, "Whenever someone says `I don't know,' I always know that they know." Upon hearing this, the person usually gets hit by a bolt of insightful lightning, and then *admits* what he or she gets from the Agony Anchor.

Another answer we sometimes hear to the *Magic Question* is "I get nothing out of that lousy feeling." To that answer, we say to the person we are coaching, "Oh, yes you do! Now fess up and tell me exactly what you get out of having that lousy feeling." We then sit quietly and 99 percent of the time the person admits what he or she gets out of feeling the Agony Anchor.

For example, one person who came to us for Intensive Coaching[SM] said she often feels "bored." We got her to admit that she uses her negative emotion — feeling "bored" — as an excuse for being, to use her term, "lazy." Rather than exert mental, emotional and physical energy to do something exciting, she just moaned. We got her to fess up and solve her real drawback, her own laziness.

A concentrated mind will pierce a rock.

JAPANESE PROVERB

Congratulations on releasing your Agony Anchor #2: Negative Feelings and Thoughts. Now, you can de-tox your mind even more by progressing to toss out your Agony Anchor #3.

Agony Anchor #3: Distractions

Many things compete for your attention — if you allow them to. Most people are on such automatic pilot that they do not even realize they inflict these wounds on their peace of mind.

During a typical day, you could be bombarded with thousands of possible negative distractions, including

- watching the "news"
- getting overly involved in other people's crises
- interruptions
- toxic people who complain or act bothersome
- people you allow to drain your energy and time
- spending time worrying rather than taking constructive action

Why do distractions erect a huge obstacle between you and your optimism?

The reason is based in one of the most important — yet underreported — psychological realities of life:

You can have only one thought in your mind at a time. It is impossible to hold two thoughts in your head *simultaneously.*

As such, whenever you clutter your head with distractions, you make it very hard to

- focus on what you really crave to achieve in your day — or in your life
- feel optimistic

It is difficult for a beautiful flower to grow if it is being choked by weeds. In much the same way, distractions you allow in your mind feed into your Agony Anchors and do not allow your seeds of optimism to grow.

Before you can grow an optimistic approach to your life, you first need to eliminate distractions. This makes room for you to replace distractions with

- beneficial information and ideas
- time and energy to accomplish what *you* want in your life

"The happiness of your life depends on the quality of your thoughts."

Marcus Aurelius Antoninus

How To Get Rid of Your Agony Anchor #3: Distractions

Fortunately, you can reduce your distractions in a number of readily useful ways.

1. *Make A "News" Black-out*
Do not listen to the "news." Or, at least greatly limit your exposure to the "news"
- during your day
- especially just before you go to bed

Most so-called "news" really is nothing more than a ruckus rehashed over and over again. The "news" flogs your brain with tales of woe, people clamoring to join the Victim Club, and other events that have nothing to do with you succeeding in your personal goals. As such, "news" shows and reports provide a boiling cauldron of distractions that seldom really help you.

So, replace those distracting items with something uplifting and inspiring. Read something that will buoy you up, rather than bring you down. For example, you can
- read a passage of an inspiring book or magazine article
- go through the newspaper *only* reading articles whose headlines indicate you will find useful information and positive messages

For many years, your authors never have watched the evening "news" before going to bed. Instead, we read an inspiring passage of a book, inspirational quotes, and our vision statements.

It is important not to feed your mind negative information just before sleeping, such as the "news." Whatever you read or see just before sleeping can program your mood and outlook on life. So, make sure you bathe your thoughts in positive messages and images.

2. *Quiet Your Mind*

If your air-conditioner or furnace has dirt clogging up its filter, you need to clean the filter or replace it. Your mind also has a filter. If it gets clogged up with negative thoughts or distractions, you need to clean it, too.

Doing so really proves pretty easy. To do this we recommend you use this mind-cleansing three times daily, for five minutes each time:

- start of your day
- mid-day
- just before you go to sleep

Many people we coach benefit from this three-step method:

Step 1: Close your eyes. Get comfortable.
Step 2: Take a deep breath and, as you exhale, feel your body relax. Do this five times.
Step 3: Picture yourself taking a vacuum cleaner and pulling out all your bothersome thoughts, worries, bad feelings, and distractions
Step 4: Notice your mind becoming quiet. Enjoy.

3. Picture What You Want

Here is another anti-distraction technique we find helps many people we coach. You can do this

◆ every time you feel distracted
◆ as you drift off to sleep, so you can dream about what you want in your life

Step 1: Close your eyes. Get comfortable.
Step 2: Take a deep breath and, as you exhale, feel your body relax. Do this five times.
Step 3: Imagine you actually have or are doing something you really want.

For Step 3, here are a couple examples of what you might imagine:

◆ *Object* you greatly desire. For instance, if you are working hard to buy a house, the you could imagine the ideal house you are working toward owning.
◆ *Activity* you want. If you look forward to walking in a setting you adore, then you can imagine yourself walking there. Picture the sights, sounds and enjoyment you would feel as you walk in that setting.

Now, you have the picture. Go to it. Imagine what you want — and leave those distractions behind.

How To Replace Your Negative Thoughts with Positive Thoughts

Your first step toward an optimistic life is to stop feeling bothered by Agony Anchors, such as destructive blaming, negative thoughts, and distractions. We just showed you readily useful ways to delete such mental clutter and garbage.

Now, your next step is to use Positive Mind Conditioning™ methods. We will delve more into the essentials and techniques of Positive Mind Conditioning™ in two upcoming chapters.

You need to train your brain to manage your life optimistically. Positive Mind Conditioning™ flows from four key principles:

1. You can keep only one thought in your mind at a time
2. If you purposely think a positive thought, you cannot be thinking a negative thought
3. You need to train your brain to use and benefit from Positive Mind Conditioning™
4. You benefit from Positive Mind Conditioning™ by practicing its techniques over and over until it becomes a delightful habit

Positive Mind Conditioning™ is just like any skill you develop. You learned many skills. For instance, you may have learned to type, use technology, do calculations, spell, read, and more. The more you practiced those skills, the more proficiency you possessed. The less you practiced, the more rusty you became in that skill.

Your first Positive Mind Conditioning™ techniques involve de-toxing your mind of Agony Anchors, such as blame, negative feelings, and distractions. We revealed these techniques to you earlier in this chapter. You have just begun to de-tox your mind. Now, you must start to replace those Agony Anchors to keep them away and blocked from returning into your psyche.

Your objective is to inject Positive Mind Conditioning™ into every aspect of your life. We will give you more of these techniques in later chapters.

A previous chapter gave you the five techniques that lay the foundation of achieving instant optimism. The following are more Positive Mind Conditioning™ techniques. They provide simple tips to feel upbeat moods and attitudes which are hallmarks of an optimistic person. So, it is important for you to practice these quick and easy tips each day.

Tip #1: Dwell on A Happy Situation

Think about a happy situation in your life. Imagine it over and over again in your mind. Re-live the proud, confident, cheerful mood you felt in that situation.

For example, we deliver over 100 speeches and workshops annually. Before each speech, we find it extremely helpful to get into a good mood. This helps us, and increases the likelihood the audience will enjoy and benefit from our presentation.

To accomplish this, about 15-30 minutes before a speech, we close our eyes and picture previous audiences laughing at our humor, smiling as they enjoy our audience participation activities, and thanking us afterwards for helping them. By mentally picturing such happy situations, we get ourselves into the same optimistic mood we felt before. Then, when we greet our audience and deliver our speech, as Yogi Berra remarked, "It's like *deja vu* all over again!"

"We become what we habitually contemplate."

GEORGE RUSSELL

Tip #2: Listen to Upbeat Music

You undoubtedly hear certain music and immediately feel a sense of delight. The music probably evokes a fond memory. Perhaps you heard that music while doing something you particularly enjoy doing. Or maybe that music came out at a special time in your life.

Both of us created "customized" audiotapes containing our 10-12 favorite upbeat songs. We listen to them anytime we want to boost our moods and our energy. In fact, we notice we usually start feeling better the instant the music begins to play.

Homework: List about 10 music pieces that evoke delight in you. Obtain copies of the music, and make an audiotape containing all the music. For example, one person we coached listens to her "customized" music tape each time she wants to get into a fantastic mood to do a project or go to a special social event.

"I don't sing because I'm happy.
I'm happy because I sing."

WILLIAM JAMES

Tip #3: Laugh

Humor is good medicine. Lee Berk, M.D., and Stanley Tan, M.D., of Loma Linda University found laughing produces wonderful benefits.[1] It helps you

- ◆ lower your blood pressure

- boost your immune system
- decrease your damaging stress hormone production
- unleash your flow of beta endorphins, your body's chemical that leave you feeling euphoric

"Humor is the great thing, the saving thing. The minute it crops up, all our irritations and resentments slip away, and a sunny spirit takes their place."

MARK TWAIN

Homework: Make a list of books, magazines, films and TV shows you find funny. Indulge your sense of humor. In fact, Norman Cousins in his *Anatomy of an Illness* book recounts how laughing each day helped him fight life-threatening illnesses.[2]

"He who sings frightens away his ills."

CERVANTES

Tip #4: Start Your Day with Enthusiasm

Jump out of bed quickly, and say something like "I'm going to do great today" over and over. We find this especially helpful when we have a busy day planned. By starting with enthusiasm, you immediately experience the Latin phrase *Carpe Diem* — "Seize the Day."

"Nothing great was ever accomplished without enthusiasm."

Ralph Waldo Emerson

Tip #5: Do Any Exercise

Exercise, especially aerobic exercise, is a proven way to boost your mood and decrease stress, according to Tedd Mitchell, M.D., medical director of the renowned Cooper Wellness Program in Dallas.[3] This occurs, according to Dr. Mitchell, because exercise helps the body discharge adrenaline, a stress-producing chemical.

In fact, Deepak Chopra, M.D., author of *Ageless Body, Timeless Mind,* reports exercise lifts depression and prolongs youthfulness.[4] This illustrates how a little movement can help you emotionally. Many people hesitate to actually do aerobics. So, instead, you can do almost any type of movement, and it will help lift your spirits.

In fact, we find that even just 15 minutes of movement — walking, push-ups, climbing stairs, or anything — produces a sense of greater

◆ calmness
◆ clear-headed thinking
◆ energy
◆ confidence
◆ good health

Here are some ways to squeeze exercise into typical activities you do everyday:

Do This Movement	Instead of ...
Climbing stairs	Taking elevator
Standing while talking on phone	Sitting
Walking	Driving
Parking at far end of parking lot	Parking nearby
Mall walking	Watching TV at home
Using exercise machine	Being couch potato

Tip #6: Keep A Journal

Psychotherapists often suggest keeping a journal in which you write down your "feelings." Our professional experience shows this sort of journal writing is too vague and not focused enough to help. Fortunately, we developed a more concrete journaling method that proves helpful. Here's how you can do it.

Fifteen minutes before going to bed, write in your journal. Each journal entry should *list* the following:

1. Your day's
   A. Positive events
   B. Negative events
2. Actions you took that resulted in your day's positive events.
3. Things you can do differently or better to rid your life of the negative events.
4. Things you feel grateful for — actions or events that contribute to you feeling grateful you are alive.

We recommend you end your journal entry by focusing your thoughts on things or people you feel grateful for. This type of focus on gratefulness is an instant mood lifter, and instills hopefulness and inspiration.

"Gratitude is not only the greatest of virtues,
but the parent of all the others."

CICERO

Our clients continually tell us that our brief, organized journal writing method helps them

- ◆ reduce stress
- ◆ boost happiness
- ◆ increase positive events and decrease negative events
- ◆ feel heartfelt gratitude

Homework: Keep a daily journal using the following outline.

Sample Journal Page

Today's Positive Events	My Actions That Led To My Day's Positive Events
A.	A.
B.	B.
C.	C.

Today's Negative Events	Actions I Can Take To Rid My Life of These Negative Events
A.	A.
B.	B.
C.	C.

Things I Feel Grateful for Today

A.

B.

C.

D.

Summary: 4 Secrets To Optimism

Optimistic people

1. Cut agony anchors that hold them in the past, including
   - blaming others and themselves
   - negative feelings and thoughts
   - distractions

2. Use the five 60-second optimism methods (see Chapter 2)

3. Continually use Positive Mind Conditioning™ techniques, including methods you learned in this chapter (and upcoming chapters)

4. Discover their most heartfelt aspiration in life, and then spend most of their time pursuing it.

   Do you know what is your life's most heartfelt aspiration? To find out, go to the next chapter...

5

Discover Your Inspiring "Vision" For Your Life

*"Vision is the art
of seeing things invisible."*

JONATHAN SWIFT

Optimistic people do what they really love doing. This fills their lives with excitement. They discovered their inspiring vision that motivates them to enjoy life and feel fulfilled.

"Successful people have vision,
unsuccessful people have fantasies."

MICHAEL W. MERCER

Let's look at the other side, too. Think of some people you know who feel depressed, pessimistic, or like an accident-about-to-happen. Such people — and there are millions — tend not to know exactly what they want to do with themselves. They seem like lost souls. Their despondency results from them not possessing a fabulous reason to get out of bed and greet the day.

As such, a key step in your march to an optimistic lifestyle is for you to discover precisely what purpose motivates you, turns you up, and turns you on every single day.

This goes way beyond goal-setting. This requires digging deeply into your heart to find what fuels your fire for life.

We find many well-meaning people write their goals *before* they find out what their exciting "vision" or purpose in life is.

However, we find in our Intensive Coaching℠ sessions that people who are happy and optimistic create a vision *before* they establish their goals.

*"Without a vision, goals are useless and
misdirected — because they are not a true
reflection of your worthy purpose."*

Maryann V. Troiani

In research for his book *How Winners Do It: High Impact
People Skills for Your Career Success*, Michael uncovered a fascinating difference between underachievers and high-achievers.[1] Specifically, underachievers tend to decide what to do
each day using a three-step method: Ready - Fire - Aim!

In contrast, high-achievers — winners in life and in their
careers — use a different three-step method. They use the
Ready -Aim - Fire approach.

Now that you rid yourself of your Agony Anchors (see
the previous chapter), and are setting your ship out to sail,
your ship cannot sail in the right direction until you decide
exactly where you want to go. So, now you need to turn on
your ship's radar. This will keep you on coarse to reach your
most desired destination.

In much the same way, your *vision* is your radar that
keeps you focused on exactly where you desire to go in your
life. Or, as we like to point out:

"If you know what you're aiming at, it greatly improves your odds of hitting your target."

MICHAEL W. MERCER & MARYANN V. TROIANI

8 STEP METHOD TO DISCOVER YOUR INSPIRING "VISION"

To help you find exactly what you most want to aim at in your life — your *vision* — we developed and perfected an enjoyable and easy eight-step procedure. Please complete each step as you read about it. By the end of this chapter, you will have a clear, exciting, practical vision statement. Plus, you then will be ready to benefit from our next chapter on how to set goals that enable you to achieve your very most heartfelt desires.

"The secret of success is consistency of purpose."

BENJAMIN DISRAELI

We realize some readers prefer to think in a "left-brain" (logical, fact-focused) manner, while others of you like "right-brain" (intuitive, feeling-focused) thinking. And some of you use both sides of your brain. We want all of you to profit from our well-honed vision creating method. So, we will give both right-brainers and left-brainers methods to pinpoint precisely what really drives you to enjoy a meaningful, exciting, cheerful life. Specifically, each step includes two ways to complete it:

◆ written method (left-brain, logical focus)
◆ visualization method (right-brain, intuitive and feeling focus)

You can use whichever way you most enjoy using, or use both. Your outcome will be the same: You will arrive at your clearly stated *vision* to help you live a healthy, prosperous, and happy life.

"If one advances confidently in the direction of his dreams, and endeavors to live the life which he imagined, he will meet with a success unexpected in common hours."

HENRY DAVID THOREAU

Finally, after each step you can read about Maryann completing that step. Her example will help you gain even more understanding of how to do the step in a useful manner. When Maryann was considering her own career changes she used this eight-step process which she found inspiring. She felt it gave her direction and also insight into why she desired a change in her career from a hospital program director to an "Intensive Coach," speaker, and book author.

Step 1: Your Positive Traits

Your first step on your journey to pinpoint your inspiring vision for your life is to make a list of your positive traits. You can do this on a piece of paper or on notecards. Importantly, only list your absolutely fabulous, wonderful, admirable characteristics. It will not help you to write your less praiseworthy attributes.

Here is a list of some positive traits. You can choose from this list. However, this is not a complete list. It just gives you a partial list to stimulate your thinking. Feel free to list any other traits you feel proud of.

Partial List of Positive Traits

Adoring	Funny	Logical
Adventurous	Giving	Loving
Ambitious	Happy	Loyal
Attractive	Hard-working	Orderly
Brave	Helpful	Organized
Caring	Honest	Patient
Cheerful	Humility	Persistent
Confident	Humorous	Persuasive
Considerate	Imagination	Playful
Courageous	Industrious	Resourceful
Creative	Innovative	Sincere
Enthusiastic	Integrity	Supportive
Exciting	Intuitive	Thrifty
Faithful	Joyful	Tolerant
Friendly	Kind	Trustworthy

Visualization #1

Get into a relaxed state by closing your eyes, taking a few deep breaths, slowly exhaling each breath, and releasing all tension from your body.

Once relaxed, with your eyes closed, picture or imagine a moment or situation where you felt really magnificent about yourself.

What were your positive traits at that time? Take some time to fully appreciate your positive traits then. When you open your eyes, take a piece of paper, and jot down your positive traits.

Example

For example, when Maryann completed this step, she listed the following as her positive traits:

◆ Adventurous   ◆ Giving
◆ Caring   ◆ Loving
◆ Considerate   ◆ Nice
◆ Courageous   ◆ Persistent
◆ Creative   ◆ Playful
◆ Enthusiastic   ◆ Supportive
◆ Faithful

Step 2: Activities You Like To Do

Make a list of activities you enjoy doing. Only include activities that really light your fire. These are activities you cherish performing. Your list even can include activities you did only once or twice, but incredibly relished.

The following is a partial list of activities you may enjoy. Of course, use this list to spark your thinking about the most delightful activities you engage in.

Partial List of Activities People Enjoy

Administrating	Helping people	Reading
Baking	Influencing	Repairing
Building	Innovating	Selling
Communicating	Inventing	Serving
Computer work	Investigating	Shopping
Creating	Leading	Singing
Dancing	Learning	Speaking
Dismantling	Managing	Teaching
Drawing	Meditating	Traveling
Driving	Negotiating	Walking
Engineering	Persuading	Working with people
Exercising	Playing music	

Visualization #2

Get into your relaxed state.

Picture or imagine an activity you really enjoyed doing. Give yourself time to savor your actions.

Then, open your eyes. Write down those activities.

Repeat this visualization exercise for two other activities you relished doing.

Example

Below are Maryann's list of activities she greatly enjoys doing:
- Dancing
- Exploring
- Giving
- Guiding
- Influencing
- Leading
- Learning
- Speaking
- Teaching
- Working with people

Step 3: Your Proudest Accomplishments

List your achievements you feel proudest of. These could be accomplishments in any area of your life. For example, you might list proud accomplishments like
- being highly successful in an endeavor
- buying a house
- developing a great relationship
- earning a certain amount of money
- earning a degree
- learning a new skill
- owning an item you prize
- paying off your debts
- raising healthy children

Visualization #3

Get into your relaxed state.

With your eyes still closed, visualize a moment you felt incredibly proud of yourself. Create a vivid picture of this moment and re-experience your positive feelings and thoughts. Enjoy this for a couple minutes. Then, open your eyes. Write down your incredible achievement you visualized.

Repeat this visualization method for as many achievements as you desire.

Example

When Maryann listed her proudest accomplishments, she felt it was "really eye-opening...a *WOW* experience." She listed the following achievements:

- becoming mental health director of an insurance company
- becoming program director at major psychiatric hospital
- co-authoring books
- creating wonderful love relationship
- earning doctoral degree
- finding the love of her life
- graduating from college
- growing a business to the point she could sell it
- passing psychologist licensing exam
- paying off all student loans
- special relationships with nieces and nephews

Step 4: What You Want To Be Remembered For

Take a moment to reflect on the following question: What do you want to be remembered for in your life in terms of your *outstanding* traits and achievements. These can be qualities and achievements you already have achieved and listed in Steps 1 and 2. Or, you can include traits and accomplishments you aim to achieve in the future.

Jot down two lists. One list is composed of your life's exceptional traits. Your second list tells of your chief accomplishments.

Visualization #4

Get into your relaxed state.

With your eyes still closed, imagine you already passed on from this world, and someone wrote a story about outstanding things you did in your life. In your mind, read this story. What does the story say about you? What does the story tell the world about your

- ◆ Positive traits
- ◆ Accomplishments

Relish your wonderful story with enthusiasm. Soak it in. When you are ready, open your eyes. Write down your two lists.

Example

For these two lists, Maryann listed the following as traits and accomplishments she wants to be remembered for in her life:

<u>Outstanding Traits</u>	<u>Outstanding Accomplishments</u>
Caring	Being a doctor
Creative	Co-author of best-selling books
Enthusiastic	Fabulous love relationship
Giving	Helped many, many people
Influential	vastly improve their lives
Inspirational	Well-known psychologist
Loving	
Supportive	
Unforgettable	

Step 5: People You Admire

People have fun answering this question: Whom do you tremendously admire? You can focus on people you know or people you have read about. For each person you admire, what specifically do you admire about this person in terms of his or her outstanding

◆ Positive traits
◆ Actions and accomplishments

In previous steps, you listed your positive qualities and accomplishments. Now, you get to list the outstanding traits and achievements of the people you hold in high esteem.

Visualization #5

Get into your relaxed state.

With your eyes closed, imagine a person you tremendously admire. Conjure up a mental picture of that fantastic individual. See that person doing what you admire him or her for. As you watch this person in action, observe their positive traits and accomplishments. Notice what the person is doing and how they go about doing it. Finish up this scene and open your eyes. Take a piece of paper. Write two lists, one for the person's positive traits and another list of the person's achievements. Then, repeat this visualization method for other people you greatly admire.

Example

Maryann most admires these positive traits, actions and accomplishments of three prominent people.

Person #1: Famous Singer/Actress

<u>Positive Traits</u>	<u>Actions & Accomplishments</u>
Influential	World famous
Inspirational	Best-selling albums
Persistent	Dynamic singer
Timeless	Great dancer
Flexible	Groundbreaking videos
Creative	Innovative writer
Special	Moving speaker
Intelligent	Teacher
Powerful	Mentor
Courageous
Ambitious
Hard-working
Unforgettable

Person #2: Famous Artist

<u>Positive Traits</u>	<u>Actions & Accomplishments</u>
Flexible	Internationally recognized
Inspirational	Trend-setter
Daring	Best in her field
Talented	Admired
Innovative	Teacher
Poised	Mentor
Unforgettable

Person #3: Talk Show Host

Positive Traits	Actions & Accomplishments
Influential	Nationally famous
Inspirational	Best in field
Persistent	Widely admired
Creative	Trend-setter
Special	Makes big impact on people
Intelligent	Speaker
Powerful	Motivating teacher
Ambitious	Mentor
Hard-working	
Courageous	
Confident	
Innovative	
Charismatic	
Unforgettable	

Step 6: Find Your Patterns

Question: Now, what do you do with your lists from Steps 1 -5?

Answer: Find the common threads, themes, or patterns that appear in your lists.

How do you do this? First, take two pieces of blank paper. On one piece of paper, put the heading *"Positive Traits."* On the second sheet, write the heading *"Actions & Achievements."*

Second, put both pieces of paper in front of you.

Third, review the lists you made in Steps 1 - 5. Write *repeated* words, phrases, and ideas from your

♦ positive trait lists in Steps 1, 4A, and 5A
♦ actions and activities you most enjoy and admire, based on your lists in Steps 2, 3, 4B, and 5B

Remember, you need to spot commonalities.

Fourth, take your two lists and circle your top
- ◆ two positive traits
- ◆ two favorite actions and achievements

These must be the positive traits plus actions and achievements that you consider most personally valuable and — definitely — heartfelt.

Example

If you looked at Maryann's two lists, you would find the common threads or repeated words, patterns and ideas listed below. The circled ones are her most heartfelt and valued.

<u>**Positive Traits**</u>

Inspirational

Influential

Creative/Innovative

Unforgettable

Persistent

Enthusiastic

Courageous

<u>**Actions & Achievements**</u>

Best in field

Nationally famous

Makes big impact on people/
   helps people

Trend-setter

Speaking/Teaching

Mentor

Step 7: Your Inspiring Vision Statement for Your Life

The purpose of your vision statement, as we described earlier, is to turn on your ship's radar. Your vision statement pinpoints your most heartfelt aspiration. Plus, by using your vision statement, you definitely will spend each day taking actions to move your life in the direction you most deeply desire. Your vision statement helps you
- ◆ focus on what you consider most important
- ◆ radiate specialness

- ◆ awake each day with excitement about taking actions to achieve your most heartfelt desires
- ◆ feel enthusiastic, alive, and spirited
- ◆ be in-control

"Successful people aim for the stars, whereas average people just aim to keep their feet on the ground."

MICHAEL W. MERCER & MARYANN V. TROIANI

Remember what we said earlier in the book. Research, our personal experiences and insights from Intensive Coaching[SM] sessions we do with clients clearly show that optimistic people feel in control of their lives, special, excited, and enthusiastic.

"How many cares one loses when one decides not to be something but to be someone."

COCO CHANEL

And, very importantly, successful people endeavor to spend 23 hours and 59 minutes each day focused on what they most want — not on what they do not want. Your vision statement helps you do this.

Using your final list of your two top positive traits and two favorite activities and actions (from Step 6), you readily create your heartfelt vision statement by filling in the following phrase:

I am a/an [2 *positive traits*] [2 *of your favorite activities or actions*].

Example

As you can see, Maryann's vision statement appears as the following:

I am an inspirational and influential speaker and mentor.

Using this seven step method, Maryann discovered her ultimate purpose in life and what makes her feel supremely motivated.

Start Your "Vision Card"

A convenient way to stay focused on your inspiring vision is to read your vision statement a few times each day. Doing so readily reminds you of what you consider ultra-important.

To do this, we recommend you make a *Vision Card*. Start it now by typing or printing your vision statement.

In upcoming chapters, you will add other crucial optimism ingredients to your Vision Card. By the time you finish this book, you will have a small yet immensely useful Vision Card you can carry everywhere. Reading it a few times daily keeps you on-target toward the healthy, prosperous and happy life you make for yourself.

Importantly, during Intensive Coaching^{SM} sessions we conduct, we always notice that when our clients create their vision statements, they react like someone who just discovered a magnificent treasure.

And now you also have discovered your treasure.

"A strong will, a settled purpose and an invincible determination can accomplish almost anything; and in this lies the distinction between great men and little men."

THOMAS FULLER

6

Turning Your Vision Into Reality

*"The ability to convert visions to things
is the secret of success."*

HENRY WARD BEECHER

In the last chapter, you conceived your vision statement for what you most want to do with your life. That is great.

However, your vision statement will not be worth the piece of paper you wrote it on — unless you turn your vision into reality. We find optimistic people live their vision. That accounts for much of the reason they feel so upbeat, enthusiastic, and alive.

How do you do this? We will teach you how to turn your vision into goals. The methods we will suggest to you are proven effective. We use variations of these procedures in workshops we deliver, as well as Intensive Coaching^{SM} sessions with our clients.

"Destiny is not a matter of chance,
it is a matter of choice;
it is not a thing to be waited for,
it is a thing to be achieved."

GEORGE BERNARD SHAW

As we stated in the last chapter, we realize some of you think in a left-brain (logical, fact-focused) manner. Others of you prefer right-brain (intuitive, feeling-focused) thinking. Since we want all our readers to benefit from this experience, we will give you both left-brain and right-brain methods. You can use all the procedures described in this chapter. Or, you can pick and choose the techniques you like best. Regardless of how you use this chapter, make sure you conclude this chapter with your most heartfelt goals clearly written.

And now your adventure begins . . .

How To Pinpoint Precisely What You Want

Take some time to work on the following questions and visualization exercises. These will help you further evaluate precisely what you most want or desire. Doing so will lead you to establish your goals that you will feel excited about pursuing.

Visualization Exercise

Get into your relaxed state. Read the following questions. Then, answer them with your eyes closed.

Question #1: Imagine or picture what you would most like to have in your life? What would you like to *improve*? What would you like to change in your life? Write down your responses to these questions.

Question #2: Keep in mind your responses to Question #1. Imagine how you would feel if it was five years from now, and you still have not brought into your life what you most want to have, improve, and change. What emotions does that conjure up in you? Write down these emotions.

Question #3: Ask yourself, "Why have I not already accomplished these things before?" Many people we coach respond that they

- ◆ never thought about wanting these items, improvements, or changes
- ◆ never worked enough on these desires
- ◆ felt afraid to do things differently
- ◆ held on to many excuses and their Agony Anchors (see previous chapter entitled, *De-tox Your Mind)*
- ◆ lacked knowledge, skills, or abilities
- ◆ admitted they really did not want it very badly

Question #4: If you could do, have or be anything you want in life, what would that be? Imagine your perfect existence. You also can achieve this fabulous state-of-affairs by imagining you reached your heartfelt vision.

Describe on paper the perfect scenario you just imagined. Write the details of what you are doing, feeling, and seeing in your perfect existence.

Question #5: Ask yourself, "What is *ultra-important* to me? What most matters to me?"

The reason we include these questions is that in our Intensive Coaching^{SM} sessions we found some people, when they answered these questions, felt like they were hit by a bolt of lightning. For example, what they answered is ultra-important to them is not consistent with their most desired actions and achievements (discussed in previous chapter).

For example, one woman we coached wanted to expand her business and felt that this was her top desire. However, after she answered this question she felt startled. She discovered that to pursue building her business would take her away from spending time with her children. What most mattered to her was to provide her children with guidance and time. Thus, she had two competing desires and priorities. Her solution: Build her business 50 percent of the time and balance that with spending the other 50 percent with her husband and children. This solution worked perfectly. Her balance of time and attention gave her more energy to focus on building her business, because she released her Agony Anchor of guilt and anxiety that she had allowed to hold her back.

Question #6: In your relaxed state, imagine everything you did during your last week. Picture all the activities you engaged in.

Then, honestly answer this question: "How much of my weekly activities actually help me move closer to achieving my vision statement?"

If you are like most people, you probably spent less than 50 percent of your time taking actions that directly help you achieve your vision. This pops up all the time in workshops we deliver and Intensive Coaching^{SM} sessions we do with clients. Why is this? Because the average person wanders through life doing whatever seems to need attention at the moment. They lose perspective of what truly is most important to them. Average people do what pops up, rather than doing what truly matters most. They are like ships sailing with their radars turned off.

Prescription: To cure this common flaw, you now are ready to transform your vision into realistic goals you will feel enthused about doing.

"If you don't know where you're going, any place will do."

ALICE IN WONDERLAND

Steps To Turn Your Vision into Realistic Goals

Step 1: List two to four specific accomplishments or actions you need to complete to progress toward achieving your vision. These specific accomplishments or actions become your goals. In general, your goals must include specific measures and deadlines.

You can choose only two to four goals to work on to achieve your vision. At least one of your goals must be a goal to "balance" your life. Balancing your life helps you find the energy and support to achieve your vision.

Your goals can be from one or more of these six categories:

- ◆ Health & Physical Condition
- ◆ Work/Career
- ◆ Emotional/Mental Health
- ◆ Money/Financial
- ◆ Spiritual/Creativity
- ◆ Personal, such as relationships, family, interests, and hobbies

It is really easy to write a useful goal. It boils down to just including four ingredients in each goal you write:

- ◆ Verb or action
- ◆ Measure or quantitative amount
- ◆ Subject of goal
- ◆ Deadline date

"Give me a stock clerk with a goal, and I will give you a person who will make history. Give me a person without a goal, and I will give you a stock clerk."

J.C. PENNEY

Example

In the previous chapter, we showed you examples of how Maryann arrived at her Vision Statement. Now, you will see goals she created that help her progress toward her heartfelt vision. The following table shows her goals using the four ingredients:

Verb	Measure	Subject	Deadline
Give	20	speeches	by December
Get quoted & interviewed	50 times	on TV, Radio & newspapers	by December
Coach	10	new clients	by December
Practice	good	health habits	each day

Now, it is your turn. Take a piece of paper. Write up to four goals that will move you toward your vision. Do not include any goals that cloud your vision. Remember: You should include a goal that promotes "balance" in your life.

Step 2: Make sure your goals help you move toward your vision. To do this, you will find it helpful to evaluate your goals in a few areas.

First, on a scale of 1 - 10 (1 = little, 10 = a lot), how proud would you feel when you complete the goal. Only keep goals on which your pride level would be 8 - 10. You will feel immensely motivated knowing your goal accomplishment boosts your self-respect.

Second, how much would the goal help you progress toward your vision? Again, use a 1 - 10 rating scale. Keep goals that you rate 8 - 10. After all, since your vision is ultra-important to you, why would you settle for anything less?

Third, refer to Step 6 in how you created your Vision Statement (see previous chapter). A useful goal helps you

◆ use your positive traits
◆ work on your most desired actions and achievements

Finally, list who you will use as your cheerleader and advisor on each goal. You will find it easier and more delightful if you bring such people into your work on each goal.

A *cheerleader* is someone who may not be an expert on how to achieve one of your goals. But, your cheerleader definitely is someone who encourages you, thrills in your successes, and makes a fuss over you when you do well. Your cheerleaders can be your spouse, partner, friends, and family members.

In contrast, an *advisor* possesses expertise in your goal. For instance, if you want to improve a skill, your advisor may be a teacher or someone who already exhibits the know-how you want — and will tell you how to do it, too.

Example

Here is how Maryann evaluated her four goals using our goal evaluation model.

Goal	Pride 1 - 10	Vision 1 - 10	Progress Toward Positive Traits	Desired Actions	Cheer-leaders & Advisors
Give 20 speeches by December	10	10	Persistence Inspirational Influential	Helps people Speaking Teaching Courageous	Mike Mentor
Get quoted 50 times on TV, radio & in newspapers by December	10	10	Creative Unforgettable Influential Giving	Helps people Speaking National fame Teaching Enthusiastic	[famous author] Mike
Coach 10 new clients by December	10	10	Influential Inspirational Enthusiastic Caring Supportive	Helps people Mentor Teaching Guiding Giving	Abbey
Practice good health habits each day	10	9	Creative Persistent Enthusiastic	Balance	Paulette Mike

Now, it is your turn. You want to make sure your goals help you move in the right direction. So, spend a little time evaluating your goals. We suggest you discard any goal that does not help you tremendously. Also, make sure you find cheerleaders and advisors soon for each goal where you may not have them yet. Go to it.

Step 3: Rank-order your goals. You probably do not feel all of your goals are equally valuable to you. For that reason, rank your goals, as follows:

- ◆ 1 = Most important to you
- ◆ 2 = 2nd most important
- ◆ 3 = 3rd most important
- ◆ 4 = 4th most important

Ranking your goals give you a clear sense of your priorities.

> *"Things which matter most must never be at the mercy of things which matter least."*
>
> GOETHE

Step 4: List your weekly actions. The simplest and most direct way to achieve your goals is to take actions each week to progress on your goals. You do not need to work on each goal every day. But each day you should take at least one action on at one or more of your goals.

Keep in mind that one hallmark of pessimistic people is they often spend an entire day doing nothing on any of their most important goals. And then they wonder why they feel downhearted and unaccomplished!!

"Without action, a person's exciting vision is solely a daydream."

Maryann Troiani

Example

The following shows you how Maryann plans weekly actions on one of her four goals: *Practice good health habits each day.* Each week, Maryann takes these actions:
- Exercises 4 times/week
- Eats healthy meals each day
- Takes vitamins
- Meditates 15 minutes each day
- Takes relaxing walk 3 times/week

Now, it is your turn. You can use the following format for each of your goals:

	Goal 1	**Goal 2**	**Goal 3**	**Goal 4**
Monday				
Tuesday				
Wednesday				
Thursday				
Friday				
Saturday				
Sunday				

Add To Your "Vision Card"

To help you conveniently keep track of your goals, add them to your *Vision Card*. In the last chapter, we suggested you take paper or a card and type or print on it your Vision Statement. Now, add to your *Vision Card* your

◆ Goals
◆ Weekly actions to help you accomplish your goals

Congratulations!! You have good reason to feel more optimistic. You have created your Vision Statement, plus goals and weekly actions so you will progress toward your exciting vision.

Hold on to your hat! In the next chapter, we will serve as your advisors and cheerleaders to help you

◆ motivate yourself to achieve your vision
◆ release more Agony Anchors or obstacles
◆ experience Positive Mind Conditioning™

7

Positive Mind Conditioning™ - Part I:

5 Essentials

In our studies of optimistic people — and our unique Intensive Coaching^SM sessions to help people boost their optimism — we discovered key methods they use to stay ultra-motivated. This motivation fuels their ability to accomplish their goals and, ultimately, attain their vision. We will show you these methods so you can put them into action to become more healthy, prosperous, and happy. We call this *Positive Mind Conditioning™*. Importantly, these are totally learnable techniques and skills. You do not have to be born this way. Also, you do not have to worry that it is too late in your life to grasp it. All you need to do is practice these skills each day so you can benefit. You will learn five essentials of making yourself ultra-motivated.

5 Essentials To Feel Ultra-Motivated To Achieve Your Vision & Goals

You can supercharge your motivation when you use the five essentials underlying all motivation, ambition, and drive.

These elements form the foundation for you continuously feeling motivated.

To benefit, simply keep these essentials in mind all day every day. Eventually, they will turn into beneficial habits. They enable you to maximize your power to achieve whatever you set out to do. Importantly, using these essentials also help you work smarter, not harder. With them, you harness your mental energy to complete tasks quicker and in a more creative, positive manner.

Nothing is impossible to a willing mind.

FRENCH PROVERB

Essential #1: You Can Only Have 1 Thought at a Time

This is the key to feeling optimistic, enjoying your life, and fulfilling your vision for a delightful life. As mentioned earlier in this book, *you only can keep one thought in your head at a time.* This is one of the most powerful yet underpublicized insights in psychology.

Question: So, what should your one thought be?

Answer: Dwell on what you want to accomplish. Do not dwell on what you do not want.

This is one of the easiest ways to keep negative thoughts out of your mind. You crowd them out. After all, if you keep thinking positive, optimistic and uplifting thoughts, you cannot simultaneously focus on negative, depressing or upsetting thoughts. In fact, intriguing psychological research even shows that people who focus on positive experiences can put up with more discomfort than people who do not dwell on positive, pleasant thoughts.[1,2] Eventually, by putting this essential into action, you weed out any sprouting negative thoughts.

"Nothing contributes so much to tranquilizing the mind as a steady purpose."

MARY WALLSTONECRAFT SHELLY

To see how magnificently this essential works, do two experiments with yourself. First, the next time a negative thought crosses your path, immediately think of your vision, your goals, or a delightful experience.

Second, do random checks on your thoughts. A few times during your next five days, occasionally pause. Check to see if you are thinking pessimistic or optimistic thoughts. If you are thinking negative thoughts, you now know what to do!

Essential #2: Expect the Best

"A man is what he thinks about all day long."

RALPH WALDO EMERSON

As you begin any project, your frame-of-mind proves extremely important. It is this simple: If you start a task with a

- positive belief that you will succeed, you increase your chances that you will figure out ways to assure a successful outcome
- negative belief that you may fail, your belief makes it much harder to build up your motivation to succeed

The moral is that what you expect will materialize in reality.

"If you think you can or think you can't, you're right."

<small>HENRY FORD</small>

Let us look at it a little differently. Everyone has noticed some pessimistic people seem like an accident waiting to happen. And, lo and behold, many pessimistic, complaining people ram into all sorts of potholes.

In contrast, you probably have observed some people for whom success seems to come somewhat easily. These people almost invariably tend to be optimistic people. They *expect the best and keep their minds focused on what they want.* Through some cosmic vibrations, they draw to themselves people and opportunities that prove helpful. It almost seems like they are magnets, attracting what they want into their lives. By *constantly* expecting the best, they get exactly what they expect. So, carefully choose what you expect, because you may get it.

Essential #3: Strong Ambition

Wishy-washy people do not go very far. They get swayed by whatever crosses their paths.

In contrast, the people who move mountains, people who get things done, are people who feel a profound sense of mission. They dive into their projects with gusto. As someone once said:

Every highly successful person is a maniac on a mission.

The finest way to develop strong ambition is for you to think about your goals, ambitions and things you want many, many times each day. Again, think about what you want and specifically what you need to do to get it. This is like adding logs to a burning fire. Your intense dwelling on what you want builds incredibly strong ambition in you.

We know how powerful this method is from personal experience. As we built our businesses from scratch, we encountered many challenges and roadblocks that easily could have thrown cold water on our ambition. Using this essential method of Positive Mind Conditioning™ always gave us hope, purpose, and reason to keep plugging away. We still remember innumerable times when we kept our spirits up by smiling and saying aloud, "We're maniacs on a mission!"

Essential #4: Gumption to Change How You Think

Quite a few decades ago, one British economist was famous for holding extremely strong opinions. Once, he totally changed his opinion on an important matter. A colleague took great glee in pointing out that this opinionated economist previously held a very different viewpoint. After listening to his colleague's scorn, the economist calmly replied, "When I obtain new information that leads me to a different conclusion, I change my opinion. What do you do?"

A wise man changes his mind.
A fool never will.

SPANISH PROVERB

The way you handle situations has served you to some degree. Now, you have a tremendous opportunity to feel more confident and optimistic than you ever may have dreamed possible. To do this, we recommend you adopt or adapt some essentials of Positive Mind Conditioning™. This can unleash your energy and hone your focus on what you most want.

The difficulty in doing this is the seemingly "natural" tendency to slip back into your old ways of doing things. Some people call this a rut or the "comfort zone." Whatever you call it, you probably continually have certain habits that you would do better without. Now, you can seize your opportunity to do things a bit differently.

"To fall into a habit
is to begin to cease to be."

MIGUEL DE UNAMUNO

For example, starting now you can create a finer, more exciting future for yourself just by starting to

◆ dwell on positive thoughts of what you want —
   and avoid dwelling on negative thoughts of
   what you do not want
◆ expect the best
◆ act like a maniac on a mission

To do this, you need the gumption to change or improve some of your habitual ways of thinking.

When you hear new information on a subject, don't you sometimes change your opinion on the matter? This is similar. You can continue your habitual ways of using your brain. Or, you can inject these Positive Mind Conditioning™ methods into your daily activities. And you get to reap all the benefits of more productive ways of thinking and feeling.

"Happiness is a conscious choice,
not an automatic response."

MILDRED BARTHEL

Essential #5: Persistence

"Nothing in the world can take the place of
persistence. Talent will not; nothing is more
common than unsuccessful men with talent.
Genius will not; unrewarded genius is almost a
proverb. Education will not; the world is full of
educated derelicts. Persistence and
determination alone are omnipotent."

CALVIN COOLIDGE

Fascinating research done at Stanford University proves that persistent people achieve more than their less persistent colleagues. Psychologist Walter Mischel, Ph.D., did a research project concerning traits of four year-old children.[3] In this project, a researcher met in a room with each four year-old being studied. The researcher showed each child two marshmellows, and told the child that upon completing certain tasks the child could eat both marshmellows. Since small children adore marshmellows, the marshmellows represented a big treat. The researcher put the marshmellows on the table where the researcher and child sat, within easy grasp of the four year-old.

At one point, as planned, the researcher told the child that she needed to leave the room for 15-20 minutes, and that the child should stay in the room. Unknown to the children, they were being watched through a one-way mirror.

Some children — those with limited impulse control — grabbed the marshmellows and ate them while the researcher was away.

However, other children — kids who delayed gratification — did not touch the marshmellows. They diverted their attention to other activities in the room. Sometimes they looked at the marshmellows with hunger in their eyes. But these children never touched or ate the treats.

As such, Dr. Mischel collected data on two types of children, those who exhibited

1. desire for immediate gratification
2. persistence to wait until they earned their treat, that is, children who delayed gratification

But that is not all. A dozen to 14 years later, researchers followed up on the children. The children then were 16 - 18 years-old and attending high school. Fascinating findings popped up.

The children who had exhibited the ability to persist and delay gratification, stood out as much more competent human beings than the children who grabbed the marshmellows. The children with persistence were more

◆ socially competent
◆ assertive
◆ confident
◆ likely to pursue challenges
◆ able to handle frustrations

♦ likely not to give up when encountering obstacles
♦ willing to start and complete projects

And that is not all. These persistent children even earned higher grades in school! This is especially fascinating, since there was no significant difference in IQ scores between the impulsive and persistent children!!

So, what can be made of this long-term research? This study shows that impulsive people are less likely to succeed in life than people who delay gratification. Or, to put it another way, people who persist achieve more than people who want their rewards before they finish a project.

You can use this information to help yourself. Successful people persist. They keep plugging away even though they may not see the *immediate* benefits or rewards of their hard work. People with stick-to-itiveness are much more likely to get what they want — eventually — than people who want it *now*.

*"Many of life's failures are people
who did not realize how close they were
to success when they gave up."*

THOMAS EDISON

An intriguing example of persistence in action occurs every year. About once a year, statistics are released about how many new businesses failed. In general, new businesses close down during their first two years of existence. Businesses that persist for two or more years are much less likely to fold.

Usually such figures are displayed to illustrate how many businesses fail. We find it more useful to put this in another light. Probably what is happening is that entrepreneurs who are impulsive and refuse to delay gratification cannot stand to keep plugging away for more than a year or two. At that point, since they have not made their fortune, they close shop.

In sharp contrast, entrepreneurs who delay gratification — who acknowledge that business success may take many years — persist. They keep focused on doing whatever they need to do to grow their businesses, although it may take them years to achieve key business goals.

"If we had no winter,
the spring would not be so pleasant.
If we did not sometimes taste adversity,
prosperity would not be so welcomed."

ANNE BRADSTREET

When we started our consulting and training businesses, a very successful businessperson told us, "It takes about five years to become successful in your own business."

As we each tackled zillions of challenges and obstacles, we often comforted ourselves with our belief that this self-made millionaire knew what he was talking about. He was right. Actually, it took us a bit more than five years to achieve the level of success we envisioned. Importantly, what would we have achieved if we had thrown in the towel too early?

The following story reflects on this point:

> The company president summoned one of his company's vice presidents into his huge, beautiful office. The president looked directly into the vice president's eyes, and said,
>
> "It's incredible how far you've gone in your career here in such a short time. After all, you were hired as a delivery person. You showed such promise that after just two months we promoted you to the position of supervisor of our entire shipping department. After working in that job for only five months, we again felt greatly impressed by you. So, we moved you into a salesperson job. Sure enough, our customers considered you a very special person to deal with. So, just three months later we promoted you to be vice president of sales. That was only four months ago. Now that I have reached mandatory retirement age, I'm leaving the company. So, I met with our company's Board of Directors to decide who should take my job as president of the company. It was decided unanimously that you should be the next president."
>
> A huge smile swept across the president's face. He held out his hand, and heartily shook the vice president's hand.
>
> The vice president proudly said, "Thanks, dad!!"

The points of this story are that, in contrast to someone who has a silver spoon put into his or her mouth, you

◆ should not expect instant gratification
◆ need to earn what you get

By disciplining yourself to keep working toward your goals until you reach them, you develop well-deserved self-esteem and confidence. These are hallmarks of every optimistic person.

"Diligence is the mother of good luck."

BENJAMIN FRANKLIN

8

Positive Mind Conditioning™ - Part II:

8 Techniques

The last chapter revealed to you the five *essentials* of our Positive Mind Conditioning™. Now, you are ready to put it into action to improve your life. To do so, you will learn eight Positive Mind Conditioning™ *techniques* that work wonders.

Technique #1: Forget Negatives in Your Past

Stop dragging yourself down with your lousy past experiences. At some point, you may as well pick yourself up, and forget parts of your past.

---

*"Dwelling on the darkness of your past
makes it hard to to create a bright future."*

Maryann V. Troiani

You can start now to free your mind to adopt a more optimistic manner. First, pinpoint exactly what experiences left a foul residue on your brain. Who made fun of you? How were you told you were worthless? Or, what did you tell yourself to put yourself down? What left you feeling like you would never learn what you need to learn? Who told you you would be a failure or someone who would not go far?

Part of developing an optimistic attitude is letting go of these Agony Anchors.

One great way to forget about your past is to use one of the essentials of Positive Mind Conditioning™. *Remember: You can keep your mind on only one thought at a time.* So, keep your thoughts on what you want in your life, not what you do not want.

For example, one woman who came to us for our Intensive Coaching^SM sessions overwhelming lived in her past. She dwelled on her past experiences — especially the troubling events — almost all the time. This person found it incredibly difficult to focus on her current life. Using Positive Mind Conditioning™ techniques, she finally released her Agony Anchors. She told us what she learned: "You can't drive ahead if you only look in the rearview mirror." Once she began to dwell on her vision and goals, she accelerated forward to heights she never before dreamed possible.

At this point, we consider it necessary to warn you about long-time methods to keep you stuck in your past: psycho-analysis and long-term introspective psycho-therapy. Decades ago, these methods originated to help people relieve emotional turmoil. Psycho-analytic therapists love to have people dwell on their past real — and imagined — upsets.

Having patients dwell on their distressing past experiences might help some people somewhat. However, spending your energy and time whining and brooding about your terrible past experiences probably will not help you now nor in your future. When you die, do you want to be remembered for the pain you complained about or your triumphs you created regardless of your past? Also, which makes you a finer role model for your loved ones, friends, and colleagues? This is a major life decision you must make.

Hint: At some point, mature people just pick themselves up by their own bootstraps and move forward.

Recommendation: *Since you can keep only one thought in your mind at a time, continually focus on your vision and goals for your exciting future.* In fact, we found from Intensive Coaching^{SM} many people that those who suffered a lot start feeling *immediate* emotional relief when they

- ◆ stop dwelling about their dreaded past experiences
- ◆ start focusing on their vision and goals for their delightful future

Technique #2: Discover How Your Role Models Think

"Don't reinvent the wheel" is often heard wisdom. You, too, should not "reinvent the wheel" as you progress. You can speed up your progress toward your vision and goals by finding role models. A role model is someone who already has succeeded in endeavors you aim to do.

For example, when Michael started his own consulting and training firm, one of his first actions was to seek out role models. He found two extremely successful professionals who had

- ◆ education similar to Michael's education
- ◆ started their consulting firms from scratch
- ◆ over a period of 15 - 20 years, developed excellent national reputations
- ◆ grew their firms into lucrative ventures

Since they were far ahead of Michael in years of experience and success, they felt no competition with him. They both gave Michael incredible advice. These tips tremendously helped him start and build his consulting and training firm.

Now, it is your chance to benefit from role models. You especially need to uncover how your role model thinks. Then, you can adopt or adapt similar thoughts into your own daily consciousness. You cannot learn this by osmosis. Just ask them. Ask questions like the following:

- ◆ "How did you devise your plans to achieve (*fill-in*)?"
- ◆ "What goes through your mind when you handle (*fill-in*) situations?"
- ◆ "What is your vision?"
- ◆ "What are your positive traits?"
- ◆ "What are your favorite activities?"
- ◆ "What are your proudest accomplishments?"
- ◆ "What thoughts help you keep on track?"

You may note these questions are somewhat akin to the questions you answered to create your Vision Statement.

From all these questions, figure out the emerging patterns or themes in how your role model thinks. For example, we did Intensive Coaching^SM sessions with a person whose vision involved becoming wealthy. That person asked the questions listed above to his role model.

His role model told him that on his road to wealth, he continually thought about prosperity, success, opportunities everywhere, and self-responsibility. Each of these continual thoughts reflected a deeply held belief or attitude, such as

- ◆ success results from following a clear vision
- ◆ prosperity will come if you set and achieve your goals year after year
- ◆ opportunities pop up everywhere, as long as you keep your eyes open; sometimes opportunities are right under your nose
- ◆ self-responsibility means saying, as the proverb goes, "If it is to be, it is totally up to me"

Homework: What are your role models' thoughts, beliefs, and attitudes? Discovering these facts can speed up your progress. So, find out soon.

Technique #3: Associate with Winners

"I would rather be on the side of those who believe anything possible."

AMELIA EARHART

To a large degree, you become like the people you hang around with. If you hang around with underachievers, you probably will not reach your full potential. Or, if you hang around with high-achievers, you greatly boost your likelihood of succeeding, too. There are three ways you can do this.

First, seek out people who already succeeded in the arenas in which you want to succeed. Soak in their insights, ways of doing things, motivation, and zest. To determine what sorts of people you need to spend time with, just look at this chart:

If you want ...	then hang around with people who ...
fitness	exercise and lead a healthy lifestyle
wealth	attain affluence
attractiveness	take care of themselves and look good

For example, one person we coached felt an overpowering desire to be physically fit. So, she spent time with people

who exercise regularly and attend seminars on health topics. She even teamed up with a "health buddy." Her health
buddy helped her stay motivated and on-track. Plus, her
buddy was a wonderful cheerleader who made big fusses
over her physical fitness triumphs.

A second way to associate with winners is to go places
where they go. For instance, we desire to live a fine lifestyle.
One method we find helpful is to go to afternoon tea at grand
hotels. We sit there soaking in the splendid surroundings. A
certain type of energy flows through a delightful ritual like
formal afternoon tea in a charming setting. By soaking in
this spirit of gracefulness at a fine hotel, we often leave feeling inspired and like we can conquer the world.

"To have life more abundant,
we must think in the limitless terms
of abundance."

THOMAS DREIER

The third method is to read about winners. For example,
your authors love reading
- ◆ articles about successful people
- ◆ biographies of inspiring people

Such reading helps us uncover ways these "role models" act,
think, and handle situations. We aim to get at least one useful tip we can use from each article or biography we read
about these superb people. In fact, sometimes when we need

to make a decision, we ask ourselves, "How might (*person we read about*) handle this situation?"

Technique #4: Use Affirmations

An affirmation is an important type of radar to keep you on-track. It is a positive statement that points you in the direction of achieving your vision and goals. An affirmation helps you
- erase old recordings or chatter you have in your head
- record new, useful self-talk

"Your life is an expression of all your thoughts."

MARCUS AURELIUS

Importantly, each of your affirmations must
- support your vision
- be positive
- make you feel good
- be in the present tense

An affirmation is an upbeat, snappy phrase that conveys the feelings and confidence you crave to develop.

For example, one affirmation we use many times each day is "I will achieve spectacular results today!!" This affirmation supports our visions, is positive and present tense, makes us feel good, is snappy, and conveys confidence.

Here are affirmations some of our Intensive Coaching℠ clients developed and find useful each day:

- ◆ "I am prosperous."
- ◆ "I feel happy."
- ◆ "I am healthy."
- ◆ "I am physically fit."
- ◆ "People enjoy collaborating with me."
- ◆ "I am loving."
- ◆ "I feel calm."
- ◆ "I feel energetic."
- ◆ "I am healthy, wealthy, and wise."
- ◆ "I learn easily."
- ◆ "I'm getting better and better all the time."

Saturate your senses with your affirmations. You can accomplish this in three ways:

- ◆ Write and post your affirmations
- ◆ Verbalize them
- ◆ Record your affirmations

To begin with, *post* your affirmations in places you look at many times each day. Definitely, put your affirmations on your "Vision Card." Tape your favorite affirmations to your mirror, desk, or wall. Put them in your appointment book or calendar. By posting your affirmations in places you frequent, you keep exposing your mind to positive messages customized to your needs.

Also, *verbalize* your affirmations a few times each day. Repeat them aloud or to yourself. Either way, do this with enthusiasm. Verbalize your affirmations shortly after you awaken, during the day, anytime you doubt yourself, and any time you want to boost your motivation.

Finally, make a special *recording* of your affirmations. Then, you frequently can listen to them. This helps you saturate your mind even more with your positive messages.

To do this, get your recorder. Sit with your list of affirmations. As you play classical music in the background, read your Vision Statement and your affirmations into the recorder. Repeat each affirmation five times or more.

Listen to your tape each day. We especially suggest you listen to it just before you fall asleep. In fact, music therapy researchers proved that listening to tapes of music combined with positive messages actually decreases stress hormones and lifts a person's mood.[1,2] So, you benefit when you fill your mind with your delightful tape, instead of the evening "news."

Technique #5: Visualize

Throughout this book, we suggested visualization exercises you can use to discover answers to questions we posed. You also can use visualization to increase your motivation and mentally rehearse your vision and goals.

Visualization is a type of focus. Your focus can be accomplished by creating a picture, thought, belief or feeling in your mind. Choose the modes you like best. Some people like to visualize pictures and other people like to create thoughts or feelings. Regardless of the type you do, your visualizations need to

- ◆ be repeated often
- ◆ contain clear pictures, thoughts, or feelings that you are successful
- ◆ portray you as having already achieved your vision and goals

*"The thing always happens
that you really believe in, and the belief in
a thing makes it happen."*

Frank Lloyd Wright

Visualization Exercise

Here is a visualization exercise we created to help you:

Step 1: Get into your relaxed state. Then, tighten and relax each tense muscle. Go around your entire body in a full circle, tightening and relaxing each muscle. Take deep breaths while you do this.

Step 2: When your body feels peaceful, take one more deep breath. Count backward from 10 down to one. When you get to one, you should feel a deeply relaxed and hypnotic/receptive state.

Step 3: With your eyes still closed, imagine your vision as though you already achieved it. Soak in the delightful sights, sounds, and feelings. To intensify these wonderful senses, say your affirmations so they get linked to these delightful senses. Keep focused on your vision. Do not let any other thoughts creep in. Stay with your visualization for a few minutes.

Step 4: Repeat Step 3 while focusing on your goals, instead of your vision.

Technique #6: Create Your Personal "Vision Poster"

Your vision poster is a collection of pictures and "visual aids" that represent your exciting vision and goals. It is easier to reach a destination you can see than one that is hidden and out of view. By making a poster of scenes, items and experiences you will have when you achieve your delightful vision, you plan how you want to live.

This stimulates your imagination to prepare you for your future life you are actively creating. It saturates your mind with what your life will be like as you achieve your vision.

How To Create Your Vision Poster

Use these four steps to make your totally personalized vision poster:

Step 1: Buy a large poster board.

Step 2: Write your Vision Statement in the middle, and put a photo of yourself near it.

Step 3: Find pictures that represent achieving your vision. For example, you can cut out photos and drawings from magazines. Tape or glue these pictures onto your poster. Add your favorite affirmations, quotes, and inspiring phrases.

Step 4: Find pictures of rewards you will have when you achieve your vision. Attach these to your poster.

Step 5: Hang your poster in a private place. The only people who may see your vision poster are you and a "cheerleader" who is 100 percent supportive of your vision.

Look at your poster each day. Doing this imprints the images in your mind. We look at our vision posters a few times a day. Since this only takes a minute, you have no excuse not to look at your vision poster.

Technique #7: Nourish Your Mind with the Right Stuff

Constantly nourish your mind with images, ideas and information that help you achieve your vision. For example, you can

- learn more knowledge, skills and abilities you need to achieve your goals and vision
- attend workshops
- watch upbeat TV shows
- listen to instructional and motivational recordings
- read inspirational books and articles

Here is a technique we use to help program our minds to feel more optimistic. When we read an article, we underline positive words. For example, in one article we read recently, we underlined words like "accomplished," "glowing," "enjoyed," "won," and "enhancement." In the same article, we did not underline any of the negative words, such as "criticized," "upset," and "failed." By doing this, we further increased our awareness of optimistic possibilities. Plus, we practiced filtering out negative influences.

Technique #8: Practice, Practice, Practice . . .

Reading is one thing, but practice is quite different. The essentials and techniques of Positive Mind Conditioning™ work magnificently and quickly — but only when you use them.

So, we suggest you commit to our two-week Positive Mind Conditioning™ plan. This means spending the next 14 days practicing the essentials and techniques your just read.

In school, you needed to do homework to learn. Now, you need to do your "homework" to practice and perfect your optimism skills. Doing this for two weeks will get you into the habit of benefiting from Positive Mind Conditioning™ method all the time. At the end of two weeks, treat yourself to a special reward for your efforts.

However, do not stop there. It's just the beginning . . . .

"Action is the cure for melancholy."

MICHAEL W. MERCER

9

Overcoming Obstacles to Achieving Your Vision and Goals

You can train fleas! This was a popular stunt done by circus sideshows around 1900. You can do it today.

Fleas can jump pretty high. So, if you put a flea in a jar, it readily jumps high enough to escape.

So, here is how you train fleas. Put some fleas in a jar, and put a lid atop the jar. The fleas will jump up, and quickly learn they can jump only as high as the lid. After a day, remove the lid. Lo and behold, your fleas will jump only as high as where the jar's lid used to be. They will not jump out of the jar, even though they can.

You then have fleas that you know are perfectly able to jump out of the jar. But, they keep themselves "captive" in the jar — because they do not realize they have no limits.

The way you train fleas to see limits where there are none may seem a far cry from what human beings do. But, actually humans often are not very different from fleas. Like fleas, people

- ◆ think there are constraints that may not really exist
- ◆ let others "train" us not to stretch our abilities
- ◆ figure we may not make it, so why bother trying

These self-imposed limits are obstacles. Using them as crutches, we restrain ourselves from going as far as we can go.

This chapter shows you how to break through obstacles — real or imagined — that keep you down. Optimistic people do not let barriers stop them from achieving their visions and goals. They figure out ways to go above, around or through obstacles. Pessimistic people, on the other hand, tie themselves down to all sorts of real and imagined obstacles.

To start overcoming your obstacles, you first need to identify your obstacles. Your roadblocks may be two major types:

1. External obstacles, such as your job or relationships
2. Internal obstacles, for example, your limited knowledge, skills or abilities; lack of discipline; hesitancy to delay gratification; or "Can't-Do" attitude

Homework: To help yourself, we recommend you take a piece of paper, and jot a list of your external and internal obstacles. List everything you see as roadblocks to achieving your vision or completing your top goals.

Visualization Exercise

For the following visualization exercise, use your list of obstacles you just wrote. Get into your relaxed state. Close your eyes. Imagine each obstacle and how you can do away with it. Come up with many solutions for each obstacle.

Now, open your eyes. Next to each obstacle you listed, write the solutions you conjured up. Circle the solutions you definitely plan to use. Then, next to each circled solution, write the date you will begin the solution.

"Great things happen when men
and mountains meet."

WILLIAM BLAKE

7 Speedy Ways To Clear Your Roadblocks

From our research and professional experiences, we came up with the seven main barriers people face as they work toward their vision. Here, you will see the best solutions for each roadblock.

Obstacle-Buster #1: Admit Your Laziness

On one television talk show on which we were guests, the show's host posed a question like this: "Why do people stay at the same job, even if they don't like it? People are so scared and hesitant to change jobs."

We looked the host in the eye and answered,

"Because they're lazy! We bet that no one who is dissatisfied with their job wakes up in the morning and has someone hold a gun to their head while screaming, If you don't go to work, I'll shoot you!' And when these dissatisfied people arrive at work, we bet no one stands next to them with a gun while whispering in their ear, 'If you don't stay here at your job all day, I'm going to shoot you!!'"

At first, the TV show's host looked at us in total shock. Then, she started smiling as she remarked, "You're right! You hit it right on the head!!"

Then, the host explained she expected us to give the typical pseudo-humanistic drivel about how people feel oppressed and feel they *must* stay in a job they do not like. Or, it is *hard* to change jobs, so people have a right to feel pain or claim they are "victims."

But, underneath a lot of complaining are a lot of over-used excuses that boil down to nothing more than laziness. That may not sound nice to point out, but it surely is the truth.

What excuses or complaining do you use that, when you are really truthful with yourself, you would admit boils down to nothing more than pure laziness? We will not tell you what to do about it. Why? Because that would just feed into your laziness, and it is about time you started overcoming it on your own.

"He who has a why to live can bear almost any how."

FRIEDRICH NIETZSCHE

Obstacle-Buster #2: Shock Yourself

Startle yourself out of your comfort zone. Get out of the ruts you got yourself into. Sometimes when you do something new, you feel uneasy or uncomfortable. To avoid feeling uneasy or uncomfortable, you may yearn to stay in safe territory by not doing a new activity. That is your comfort zone or rut.

Imagine what your life would be like in a couple years if you did not achieve your inspiring vision and goals. If you feel o.k. with not reaching your stated vision and goals, that shows a lack of desire on your part. Or, perhaps developing your vision and goals was nothing more than a time-wasting exercise.

In contrast, if you would feel upset about not achieving your vision and goals in a couple years, then you definitely need to get in touch with your Inner Adult — and start doing something about it.

Obstacle-Buster #3: Imagine You're Dying

In the classic movie *Rocky*, an underdog pulls himself up by his bootstraps with a "Can-Do," optimistic attitude, along with tons of hard work. Rocky gets a chance to compete for the boxing championship.

His manager is a former boxer who never pushed himself hard enough to propel his own boxing career. At one point, when Rocky's confidence wanes, his manager urges Rocky not to give up. The manager says that if he — the manager — had not given up earlier in his career, then he could have made it to the top. Since he did not go for it, he will spend the rest of his life until his dying day knowing he not only did not win the championship, but he did not even have the gumption to try. That poignant moment points to the importance in your life of

- ◆ wholeheartedly committing yourself to the life you most desire
- ◆ doing whatever it takes to accomplish each goal that moves you closer to your vision for a delightful life you will feel tremendously proud of

"Of all sad words of tongue and pen,
the saddest are these:
'It might have been!'"

JOHN GREENLEAF WHITTIER

Obstacle-Buster #4: Keep Your Target in Sight

We illustrated this point on a TV talk show on which we appeared. First, we explained the importance of keeping goals in sight. To demonstrate this, we blindfolded the show's producer. We spun her around in circles a few times so she would lose track of which direction she was facing. Then, we handed her a toy squirtgun, and asked her to squirt the talk show host with the squirtgun.

Of course, she missed squirting the host each time. She was blindfolded and did not even know if she was facing in the right direction.

Then, we removed her blindfold. Within one second, she spotted the host and squirted him.

While this made a colorful talk show segment, it also illuminated an important point: *Your vision and goals are easier to achieve if you keep them in sight than if they are out of sight.*

After all, it is like the old saying, "Out of sight — out of mind!" So, how can you keep your goals in sight? That proves easy. Just use a couple methods we already recommended to you.

First, make your Vision Card, keep it with you everywhere you go, and read it often. As you may recall from previous chapters, your Vision Card is a piece of paper or index card that contains your

◆ Vision Statement
◆ Goals
◆ Actions to Take Each Week
◆ Affirmations
◆ Inspirational Quotes

Second, look at your Vision Poster each day. This gives you graphics to continually saturate your mind with the rewards you will enjoy as you progress toward achieving your vision.

As explained in the last chapter, your Vision Poster is an approximately 3-foot x 3-foot poster board. At its center is your Vision Statement with your photo. Other parts of your poster contains pictures from magazines or drawings of rewards you will enjoy as you achieve your vision. Look at your Vision Poster many times daily. Doing so constantly reminds you of the targets you are aiming at.

Looking at your Vision Card and Vision Poster each day continuously reminds you of what you consider most important. That helps you focus on crucial actions you need to take.

They also help you stay on course so you eventually hit your target. From our personal experiences and from the Intensive Coaching^{SM} sessions we do with clients, we find it is pretty hard to stray very far from goals that always are right in front of your eyes.

For example, almost everyone reading this book has flown in an airplane. When you hop on board, you fully expect the pilot eventually will land in your destination city. After all, when the airline says your plane will travel to City X, that is exactly what you expect.

But, here is a startling fact the airline never reveals to you: Over 90 percent of the time, the plane is not exactly on course! It is not precisely taking the route the pilot plans to follow to the destination. However, you never hear the pilot

- saying, "I'm too lazy to get us back on course, so I just won't"
- announcing that he does not know what to do
- deciding to fly to a different city, since that would be easier than getting back on course
- acting hysterical over being off course

You would feel appalled if the pilot flaked out, wouldn't you? You certainly would. What the pilot does is continually

- keep the destination in mind
- watch the radar and other navigational devices to help get back on course
- adjust the direction a little here and a little there so eventually the plane lands where it is supposed to

In much the same way, you benefit when you repeatedly focus on your goals. Your focus and smart work lands you at your destination.

"How unfortunate for people who give up:
They never see how close they were to
achieving their exciting vision."

MARYANN V. TROIANI

Obstacle-Buster #5: Keep Picking Yourself Up
Over & Over

When Michael did research for one of his books, *How Winners Do It: High Impact People Skills for Your Career Success**, he spent many days "shadowing" high-achievers.[1] By spending entire work days with successful people in many occupations, Michael learned first-hand how high-achievers *actually* act, think, and handle a wide variety of situations.

    One high-achiever with whom Michael spent an entire day was a tremendously successful entrepreneur. This gentleman, along with his partner, created one of the most successful ventures in their field in North America. At one point during the day, this incredibly successful individual turned to Michael and said:

---

* To obtain this book or its 6-audiotape audiobook album, see the "Materials You Can Order" section near the end of this book.

*"The only difference between winners and losers
is that winners pick themselves up exactly
one more time than losers."*

You, too, undoubtedly have fallen down or been pushed down many times. And you will fall down or fail many more times. But, imagine how much less you would be as a person if you did not keep picking yourself up "... exactly one more time ...."

*"You measure the size of the
accomplishment by the obstacles you
had to overcome to reach your goals."*

BOOKER T. WASHINGTON

To savor your proud feelings when you overcame obstacles, we recommend you invest a little time to do the following visualization exercise.

Visualization Exercise

Get into your relaxed state. With your eyes closed, imagine or picture a situation or goal you wanted to achieve, but along the way you did not succeed. Yet, somehow you picked your-self up " . . . one more time . . . " and kept plugging away until you achieved your goal. In the outcome, you felt in-credibly proud of yourself for

- achieving your goal
- showing the gumption to persist
- picking yourself up ". . . exactly one more time . . . ."

Fall seven times, stand up eight.

JAPANESE PROVERB

Obstacle-Buster #6: Give Yourself A Deadline

Imagine someone you met who possesses loads of potential but goes nowhere in life. This person may have all the brains, attractiveness, contacts or ideas needed to succeed.

Yet, this individual goes nowhere. When you ask him or her when they will finish a project or goal, the person's typi-cal response boils down to *SOT: Some Other Time!* They may reply, "Sooner or later," "Tomorrow," or "After I finish X, Y, and Z."

As you hear their excuse for the umpteenth time, you decide to act diplomatic. You avoid saying what is really on your mind, namely, "You lazy bum! You can do so much if you just got going and actually do something, rather than just talk about it!! But, you are all talk and no do!!!"

In contrast, you politely say, "Oh, I understand." How-ever, you suspect the person probably never will go very far.

Ultimately, the person will look back at his or her life and say, "Gee, I wasted a lot of my life!"

What this boils down to is that everyone needs deadlines. "Sooner or later" never comes and there always is "tomorrow." And, you *always* will have X, Y and Z (plus A - W) to do each day of your life.

If you procrastinate, you take longer than needed to reach — and enjoy — your accomplishments. What is the solution? Simply remember:

*"The best solution for
procrastination is a deadline."*

MICHAEL W. MERCER

This simple yet profound truth is why we recommend all your goals contain deadlines. Without clearly laid out, measurable goals, you do not really have a specific target to aim for. And without deadlines, you have not committed to reaching your target sooner rather than later.

Think of some proud accomplishments you missed out on, because you did not discipline yourself to meet a deadline. Perhaps you did this in your education, career, love life, relationships, or elsewhere. What did you *really* gain by taking longer than you needed? And what did you lose?

The goal will not be reached
if the right distance not be traveled.

TIBETAN PROVERB

Obstacle-Buster #7: Burn Your Bridges

A captivating tale goes like this:

A navy captain with only 100 soldiers aboard his ship was on a mission to capture an island. But, the island harbored 1,000 enemy soldiers! The captain knew his troops were vastly outnumbered. As the ship approached the island, his soldiers became frightened about being overpowered and dying. One soldier loudly announced to the rest, "If it looks impossible to win, we'll just retreat back to our ship."

The captain knew that possibility diminished his troops' desire to triumph. Their mission would flop, unless he could arouse valient fighting from his troops. So, when the ship landed, the captain got all his soldiers off the ship. Then, before anyone could stop him, he set the ship on fire. Now, the soldiers had no way to retreat. Knowing this startling reality, they mustered all their attention to brilliantly battle the 1,000 enemy soldiers. Though vastly outnumbered, they won. In doing so, they accomplished their mission they set out to do. The point of this tale is this: *Don't give yourself the option of backing out.*

A smooth sea never made a skilled mariner.

ENGLISH PROVERB

Likewise, we chatted with one highly accomplished person who ardently proclaimed, "Quitting is not an option."

To move yourself forward, you may need to burn some bridges behind you. Then, you cannot go backwards or stay stuck in your current ruts. You have no choice but to figure out how to forge ahead.

For example, Maryann needed to burn a bridge behind her to succeed in a new business. She began working on developing her new business part-time. However, at the same time, she kept her consulting business. This detracted from her time and focus, but she initially kept her consulting business for security reasons. However, her consulting business grew and became increasingly demanding. It took more time and attention away from focusing on her new venture. After awhile, she grew more frustrated and discovered that her part-time consulting business made it

- ◆ difficult to put all her time, attention and energy into her new business
- ◆ hard to grow her new business
- ◆ impossible for her to immediately follow-up on opportunities

To solve this dilemma, she sold her consulting business. As a result, she began to spend her time and energy on developing her new business. This made all the difference in the world. She began to grow her new business.

She could not have gotten that far if she did not "burn a bridge behind her." Selling her consulting business freed her of an obstacle that she previously allowed to slow her down and distract her.

"Let me tell you the secret that
has led me to my goal:
My strength lies solely in my tenacity."

LOUIS PASTEUR

A key type of "bridge" to burn entails people we call *"drainers."* These are people *you* allow to hold you back from achieving your goals.

Important: Please notice we did not write *"they* hold you back." Instead, we wrote that drainers are people *"you* allow to hold you back." Most likely, these people do not *force* you to remain tied to your past. On the contrary, *you* use drainers as one of your excuses for not progressing.

You may need to handle three types of drainers. They are people who

1. Put down your vision or goals

These are people who criticize or laugh at what you desire to accomplish. They also believe you cannot achieve your desires, and they voice disapproval and skepticism.

Man who says it cannot be done
should not interrupt man doing it.

CHINESE PROVERB

2. Act negative or constantly complain
   Such people do not share your optimistic outlook on life. Their aura of negativity drains your batteries and shoots the air out of your balloon — if you let them.

"It's not the critic who counts, nor the man who points out how the strong man stumbled or where the doer of deeds could have done them better. The credit belongs to the man who is actually in the arena, whose face is marred by dust and sweat and blood."

THEODORE ROOSEVELT

3. Try to sabatoge your success
   This involves a relationship with a friend, partner or spouse whom you consider troubling, high maintenance, or unsupportive of your vision.

   Homework: Here is a way to help you get out of the drip-drip-drip of these draining relationships:
Step 1: Write a list of the drainers in your life.
Step 2: Ask yourself, "What do they do that I allow to drain me?"
Step 3: Reflect on this question, "Do I need or want this person in my life?"

   For those people whom you cannot eliminate from your life, make a plan on how you can limit your exposure to them.

For example, perhaps you should *not* tell them about your goals.

If such drainers are family members, you may wish to limit your exposure to them. After all, you are an adult now, and you do not have to tell your mommy or daddy or other family members every single thing you do or think or plan. Limiting such information lessens the possibility of them shooting a hole in your boat.

If your drainer is a member of the Frequent Caller Club, you need to eject such telephone terrorists out of your life. So, figuratively cut the telephone cord by

◆ screening your calls
◆ not returning their phone calls immediately, so you do not reinforce them by paying attention to such behavior
◆ keeping your contact with them time-limited
◆ limiting the amount of information you disclose to them about your goals and vision

A newborn starts to become an independent human the moment its umbilical cord is cut. For many adults, the first step is figuratively to cut the telephone cord.

If your drainers are long-time friends and do not reinforce or agree with your goals in life, you can

◆ limit your contact with them
◆ find a new set of friends whose desires coincide more with yours

For example, we did Intensive Coaching^SM sessions with a man whose friends consisted of his "childhood buddies." They were friends for decades. Their chief activities together were drinking, watching sports, and complaining about their relationships and jobs.

The man realized he wanted to expand his horizons. This included changing his career, developing a magnificent love relationship, and doing productive activities in his leisure time. It dawned on him that his friends exhibited the opposite of his newly discovered vision.

In a follow-up Intensive Coaching^SM session a few months later, he told us he did not make headway on his goals until he greatly cut back on contact with his childhood friends. At the same time, he began developing friendships with people who shared visions more similar to his.

Another challenge that pops up as you become more successful is jealousy by other people. For example, after the second time we were invited to appear on *The Oprah Winfrey Show*, we ran into a long-time friend. She asked us what was new. When we briefly mentioned our upcoming appearance on *Oprah*, she looked noticeably upset. She did not congratulate us on this special accomplishment. Instead, she commented very briefly and in a disinterested voice, "That's nice, I guess." Then, she quickly changed the topic. After that incident, she acted distant and uninterested in us whenever we saw her at social gatherings. That is vastly different than the warm, friendly way she acted toward us for over 10 years!

The point of this experience is that we needed to choose between achieving our exciting visions and keeping a friend who acted jealous and unsupportive. You, too, probably will need to make such choices as you achieve your goals and move closer to your exciting vision.

Homework: Now is a good time for you to evaluate your friendships. After all, optimistic people surround themselves with people who are upbeat, supportive, and motivated.

You surround yourself with people who are . . . .

10

De-tox Your Body by Improving Your Emotions - Part I:

How Your Negative Emotions Make Your Body Sick

"The mind is a great healer."

HIPPOCRATES

If you want to make yourself sick, you can do it!

How? Just dwell on depressing thoughts, boost your anxiety, store up loads of hostility, spew forth angry tirades all the time, and dampen any glimmer of hope that creeps into your psyche.

Of course, you would be a pretty strange person to purposely foist such problems on yourself. Yet, many people take

their distressing emotions and turn them into
- ◆ illnesses
- ◆ slow healing
- ◆ increased likelihood of death

In this chapter, you will learn how to boost your health from key mind-body alliances. First, you will learn how your emotional state impacts your chance of illness. You will see this from both medical and psychological perspectives.

In Chapter 10, we will show you how to use your mind, in conjunction with physical medicine methods, to help you stay well.

In Chapter 11, you will learn techniques to help you over-come physical impediments to your optimism caused by two common but often misdiagnosed or undiagnosed physical ailments.

Importantly, insights and tips you find in this book are not meant to keep you from obtaining medical consultations. You still should see physicians and other qualified healthcare professionals. Use methods discussed in this book, as appro-priate, in conjuction with medical procedures you may need.

Health of the body is prosperity.

African (Hausa) Proverb

Research on How Your Negative Emotions Can Lead To Physical Illness

Many people intuitively feel a link exists between upsetting emotions and physical illnesses. This probably stems from the common observation that pessimistic, depressed, stress-filled and angry people seem to get sick more often than optimistic and calmer people. Plus, when people get sick, it appears that optimistic people heal or get well faster, while pessimistic or emotionally uncontrolled individuals seem to take longer to overcome ailments.

In fact, Deepak Chopra, M.D., asserts in his book *Perfect Health* that our bodies sense our moods and change accordingly.[1] For instance, optimistic or emotionally healthy feelings lead to our physiology functioning better. Or, our bodies pick up on pessimism, depression or emotionally unhealthy moods and respond by weakening our immune systems. In fact, studies reported in the journal *Psychosomatic Medicine* indicate that acute psychological stressors are linked to cellular immunity in human beings.[2, 3]

Let's delve into other evidence showing your negative moods can harm your physical health. Among the most eye-opening large-scale studies is one done by psychologist Howard Friedman & S. Boothby-Kewley.[4] Using a research technique called "meta-analysis," these researchers statistically combined results from 101 studies of how emotional mood correlates to medical illnesses.

Sure enough, this large-scale study found that people with chronic negative emotions had twice the rate of disease compared to people with healthier emotional lives. People oozing long-term pessimism, stress, hostility and hopelessness were much more likely to develop many types of ailments, including

◆ arthritis
◆ asthma
◆ headaches
◆ heart problems

Let's put this in another perspective. Everyone knows high cholesterol and smoking increase the likelihood of getting sick. Friedman and Boothby-Kewley's research discovered that chronic negative emotions are as big a medical risk factor as high cholesterol and smoking!!

Other studies also confirm the huge link between negative emotions and illness. For example, Yale psychologist Bruce McEwen and Eliot Stellar reviewed much research on the connection between anxiety and medical ailments.[5] Their findings reported in *Archives of Internal Medicine* indicate higher anxiety seems connected to

- ◆ asthma attack occurrence
- ◆ diabetes getting worse
- ◆ hippocampus harm which may decrease memory skills
- ◆ immune ability lowered
- ◆ plaque forming more (which can cause heart problems and blood clots)
- ◆ ulcer problems
- ◆ viral infections occurring more often

Additionally, as you might expect, tension can lead to headaches. Lo and behold, research supports this common observation. Health researcher S.N. Haynes and colleagues report in the *Journal of Behavioral Medicine* that when they exposed headache sufferers to prolonged stressors, headaches occurred in 83 percent of their subjects.[6]

And stress is not the only culprit. Multiple studies uncovered a significant relationship between negative feelings — such as anger and depression — and headaches.[7, 8, 9]

Amazingly, stress even makes you more susceptible to catch the common cold. For instance, a colds research team in Sheffield, England, collaborating Carnegie-Mellon University psychologist Sheldon Cohen, exposed research subjects to a virus.[10] As reported in the prestigious *New England Journal of Medicine*, 47 percent of the high-stress subjects caught the bug. In contrast, only 27 percent of the low-stress people got sick.

Worry, not work, kills a man.

MALTESE PROVERB

Negative moods, especially pessimism and depression — the opposite of optimism — also weigh heavy on the heart. Writing in the journal *Epidemiology,* health researcher Robert Anda and colleagues reported on a 12-year study of 2,832 women and men.[11] Two key discoveries are that people who

◆ continually feel pessimistic, depressed and hopeless were more likely to die from heart disease

◆ are the most depressed (three percent of all the 2,832 subjects) were four times as likely to die due to heart disease, compared to the non-depressed people

Now that you see the medical links between negative moods and medical illnesses, let's look at psychological patterns that dispose people to sickness.

Psychological Patterns of How People Make Themselves Sick

You probably notice some people get sick more than others. As psychologists, we have listened to many people describe how they happen to get sick. From our inquiries, we delineated six major psychological patterns people use to *make* themselves ill.

"If the essential core of the person is denied or suppressed, he gets sick, sometimes in obvious ways, sometimes in subtle ways, sometimes immediately, sometimes later."

ABRAHAM MASLOW

Psychological Pattern #1: Expecting to Get Ill in Certain Situations

As we explained in previous chapters, what you expect often is what you get. *You tend to attract into your life what you expect.* If you expect to get sick, you certainly may succeed!

People who do this to themselves often make statements like the following: "Everyone has a cold around here, so I'm going to get sick, too."

In contrast, Michael barely ever gets a cold or flu. And when he does start getting sick, his symptoms remain very mild and usually last only one day. He has not needed to miss any event due to illness for over 15 years!!

How does he do it? He attributes his good health to *expecting* to be healthy. As soon as he feels symptoms of a cold or flu, he *immediately* says this affirmation to himself: "I'm a totally healthy person. I will feel totally well by the end of today."

And it works!! No one can question Michael's obviously healthy results.

*"A wise man should consider that health is the
greatest of human blessing,
and learn how by his own thought to derive
benefit from his illnesses."*

HIPPOCRATES

Psycholgical Pattern #2: Setting Yourself Up To Follow Your Family's Medical Patterns

Someone with this psycholgical pattern keeps repeating an illness mantra like this: "My parents have heart disease, so I'm going to get heart disease." Lo and behold, such people often manage to follow in their family's footsteps for ailments.

However, that does not need to be the case. For example, we did Intensive Coaching[SM] sessions with one person who had a family history of heart disease. When he came to us, he reported he frequently expected to develop heart disease and die by a certain age, just like three generations of his family.

We looked at him. He was overweight, smoked heavily, and probably did not know the definition of the word "exercise." In short, he looked like he was making himself into a likely candidate for heart disease.

With our guidance, he created his Vision Statement which included a strong yearning for health. Then, he made a few goals to help him achieve his vision. His goals included healthy actions, such as

- exercising three times a week
- taking relaxing walks four times a week
- eating a healthy food plan
- meditating daily to relieve his stress

He also devised affirmations focusing on health. These included:

- ◆ "I make my heart healthy every day."
- ◆ "I am very healthy all the time."
- ◆ "I love how I look and feel after I exercise."

At a follow-up Intensive Coaching℠ session, he told us he reads his Vision Statement and goals every day, consistently works on his goals, and repeats his affirmations many times each day. He even showed us his Vision Poster. It was laden with photos of physically fit, healthy-looking men — with photos of his face taped over their faces. His poster even contained a photo of a very heathy heart that he found in a medical publication.

This person certainly was saturating himself with healthy heart goals, affirmations, and images. Importantly, he looked much healthier.

A number of years later, we received a phone call from this individual. He sounded rattled as he explained, "One of my sisters just had a heart attack. Now, everyone in my family for three generations has had a heart attack, except for me."

We asked him how he was doing. The mood in his voice suddenly rose as he proudly told us, "I feel great, and I look great. I exercise a lot and watch what I eat. My physician said I'm incredibly healthy and definitely not a heart attack candidate."

Cardiologist Bruno Cortis, M.D., a dear friend of ours and author of *Heart & Soul: A Psychological & Spriritual Guide to Preventing & Healing Heart Disease,* commends such individuals.[12] Dr. Cortis finds that "exceptional heart patients" take total responsibility for their health. They take actions to make themselves healthy.

Psycholgical Pattern #3: Getting Out of Unpleasant Commitments or Situations

To avoid doing something, you may decide to cook up an excuse to weasel out of it. What better excuse could you find than to call in sick? Even better, you could actually make yourself sick so you can have a *real* excuse and realistically cough, wheeze & sneeze when you call in sick. People who use this psychological pattern say things like

◆ "I can't help that I'm behind on that project, because I've been sick."
◆ "I can't go to your [event, party, meeting ...], because I'm sick."

Such people often do make themselves sick. Perhaps their desire to not "just say no" reflects in their immune system.

Psychological Pattern #4: Giving Yourself Permission To Take Time Off

Some individuals keep plugging away non-stop at their key endeavors. People especially do this at work or while raising children. They create hectic schedules that allow themselves no time for breaks, rest, or vacations. Then, when their non-stop churning feels like too much, they feel too hesitant, embarrassed or guilty (see Agony Anchors in an earlier chapter) to just take time off.

What's their solution? Get sick.

These individuals figure no one would dare act heartless and deny them some time off. Such individuals are prone to say, "The only time I take off is when I'm sick."

Psychological Pattern #5: Using Illness To Get Attention

This pattern is learned in childhood. If your parents show-
ered attention and caring on you when you felt sick, they
injected a mighty clear message into your brain: "When you
are ill, you immediately get lots of attention and caring. When
you're healthy, don't expect to receive nearly as much attention and care."

People who enjoy this pattern carry it into adulthood.
Often, they gravitate toward friends and mates who lavish
attention on them the moment they exhibit any illness symptoms.

What a sick way to assure you get a truckload of attention and nurturing!!!!

Psychological Pattern #6: Constipation of the Emotions

Some people feel so hesitant to express their negative emotions that they make themselves sick. Optimistic people figure out how to overcome their negative emotions. However,
pessimistic folks sometimes let their stress, depression or
anger harm their immune systems.[13, 14] There even is a branch
of medicine to study such phenomena. It is called
psychoneuroimmunology. For instance, medical researcher
Joesph C. Courtney and his colleagues studied the link between stress and colorectal cancer.[15] Their research involved
two groups: One group was 569 colorectal cancer patients.
The second group was a comparison group of people who
were similar on many factors but did not have colorectal cancer.

The researchers asked subjects how much stress they felt
on their jobs. People who said they felt extreme job-related
stress developed colorectal cancer at five times the rate of
people who said they experienced minimal job-related stress.

In other words, perhaps stored up emotions erupted physically in the form of colorectal cancer.

Similarly, the renowned cancer researcher and physician O. Carl Simonton, M.D., asserts that chronic stress suppresses the immune system.[16] This leads to a greater proneness to sickness, including cancer.

Importantly, expressing your emotions can translate to better health, as reported in a number of intriguing studies by health researcher J.W. Pennebaker and colleagues.[17, 18, 19, 20] A review of many studies researching links between expressing emotions and health support Pennebaker's results.[21] For example, in several experiments subjects were instructed to write or talk about stressful events and other feelings. These emotion-disclosing people had fewer health problems, less medical visits, superior moods and better immune system functioning than those people who did not express their emotions.

These studies point to the conclusion that if you give yourself constipation of the emotions, you could pay for it with your health and perhaps even your life. *If you don't kick out your jams, then your jams may kick you out.*

11

De-tox Your Body by Improving Your Emotions - Part II:

Methods To Help Enhance Your Health & Overcome Illness

The previous chapter showed you how pessimism and other negative emotions are linked to illnesses. It illustrated the importance of developing and constantly using optimism each day to help you
- stay healthy
- overcome medical ailments

Now, you will learn how to boost your mood to improve your health.

Your 1st Step

In *Alice in Wonderland*, Alice asks the Cheshire Cat, "Where do I begin?"

The Chesire Cat grins and wisely gives this advice to Alice: "My dear, you begin at the beginning!"

To stay or get healthy, you too need to start at the beginning. That includes making yourself optimistic. Develop a "Can-Do," hopeful attitude in which you *always* expect health in your life. To start, you can use methods we already laid out for you, including the following:

◆ Toss out your Agony Anchors
◆ Benefit from Positive Mind Conditioning™ techniques

First, review earlier chapters, especially the chapter on *De-tox Your Mind.* Your Agony Anchors may be toxic habits, such as

◆ negative feelings and thoughts
◆ blaming
◆ distractions

Get rid of those toxic "clogs" in your daily life, using the many techniques you learned in the *De-tox Your Mind* chapter.

Second, start a delightful habit of using Positive Mind Conditioning™. You read about this in two previous chapters.

———————◁◆▷———————

Remember the key:
You can have only one thought in your
mind at a time.

———————◁◆▷———————

To stay or get healthy, you need to make sure the one thought you allow in your head is positive. Each time a pessimistic, hopeless or hostile thought creeps into your mind, immediately replace it with an uplifting, useful thought. Focus on what you desire to accomplish, especially your exciting vision and goals. Avoid wasting your time dwelling on what you do not want in your life, including illness.

Now, we will show you three methods you can use right away. These methods help you tune in to health and tune out illness.

Technique #1: Health Affirmations

An affirmation is a short, snappy phrase that confidently expresses a wonderful, positive outcome you desire. As recommended earlier in this book, you benefit from repeating your affirmations a number of times each day. They help keep you on track toward achieving your vision, goals, and other delightful events you want.

A chronically sick person may dwell — probably without even realizing it — on *anti*-affirmations, like

- "I feel horrible."
- "I'm always sick."
- "I'll never get well."
- "I keep feeling worse."

Such illness expectations readily become self-reinforcing in dire ways. If you become what you tell yourself to expect, why expect illness?

Instead, to help yourself, repeatedly use positive affirmations of health each day. For instance, we told you earlier about how Michael barely ever is ill. One reason is he has repeatedly used this affirmation for well over a decade: "I am a totally healthy person."

When Michael starts feeling ill, he repeats this affirmation many times: "I will feel totally well by the end of today." He drums this into his head. Most importantly, it works.

You can do likewise. Here are some ideas for health affirmations developed by our Intensive Coaching^{SM} clients:

- ◆ "I am happy and healthy."
- ◆ "I am a totally healthy person."
- ◆ "My blood is pumping health into every cell in my body."
- ◆ "I am well."
- ◆ "I am very healthy."
- ◆ "I feel energetic."
- ◆ "I am healing my body more and more."
- ◆ "I feel healthy."
- ◆ "I am strong and healthy."
- ◆ "My body is vibrantly healthy."
- ◆ "All the cells in my body are healthy."
- ◆ "I am physically fit."
- ◆ "I feel fantastic."
- ◆ "I ooze health and aliveness."
- ◆ "My body is well and supercharged with energy."
- ◆ "I'm confident I will get better each day."
- ◆ "I know for sure I'll feel better and better."

Homework: You can use these health affirmations or create your own. Repeat your favorite health affirmations many times each day. Doing so helps boost your optimism, enhance your confidence, and nourish your seeds of health. In fact, some individuals we coach read their affirmations into a tape recorder. They play the tape anytime they want a boost.

Technique #2: Relaxation Techniques

Many people associate relaxation with goofing off or getting away from it all. That differs from what we are talking about.

Instead, there are medical and psychological reasons to get yourself into a calm, relaxed state. Relaxation may help you

- stop the development of stress-related medical ailments
- decrease tension resulting from illnesses
- stave off negative emotions that may exacerbate illness

Indeed, Daniel Goleman, Ph.D., author of the thought-provoking book *Emotional Intelligence*, reviewed research indicating relaxation assists in reducing symptoms of ailments, such as asthma, diabetes, gastrointestinal problems, and heart disease.[1] Other studies confirmed that patients with hypertension who use biofeedback-assisted relaxation show significant health improvements.[2]

You can start reaping the benefits of relaxation by using the technique laid out here. It has been used with success by Maryann to help hundreds of clients quell stress and improve their health. This method links relaxing your muscles to relaxing emotionally.

Step-by-Step Relaxation Technique

Find a quiet place with a comfortable chair, recliner, or couch. Take off your shoes. Sit with your hands on your lap and your feet flat on the floor. Loosen tight or binding clothing that prevents you from feeling comfortable. Play classical music in the background. (Note: You will learn more about using music in the next technique.) Close your eyes. Now, you are ready to start. Simply do the following steps:

Step-by-Step Relaxation Technique

Step	Focus on your...	You do this...
1	Eyes	Close your eyes.
2	Breathing	Take a deep breath through your nose and hold it. Exhale slowly through your mouth as though you are pushing the breath out of your body. Repeat 5 times.
3	Stomach	Breathe deeply from your stomach. Hold it. Exhale and feel your stomach relaxing. Repeat 1 more time.
4	Stomach	Tighten your stomach muscles. Hold it. Feel tension in your stomach muscles. Release and feel them relax. Repeat 1 more time.
5	Back	Arch your back. Tighten your lower back muscles. Hold this position. Notice the tension in your muscles. Release this posture. Notice your muscles becoming relaxed. Repeat 1 more time.
6	Right hand	Make a fist and squeeze tightly. Notice the tension. Release your fist, and notice your fingers relaxing. Each finger feels relaxed. Repeat 1 more time.
7	Right hand	Press your palm down on your lap. Feel the tension in your upper arm. Release the pressure and feel your arm relax. Repeat 1 more time.
8	Left hand	Do Step 6 with your left hand.
9	Left hand	Do Step 7 with your left hand.

10	Shoulders	Shrug or roll up your shoulders toward your ears. Feel the tension in back of your shoulders. Now, let your shoulders gently roll down and relax. Feel them become loose and relaxed. Repeat 1 more time.
11	Neck	Gently roll your head forward. Feel the tension in your neck muscles. Roll your head back up and feel your neck muscles become more relaxed. Repeat 1 more time.
12	Jaw	Clench your jaw. Notice the tension in your jaw. Now, let your jaw hang loose. Open your mouth slightly to release the tension. Relax. Repeat 1 more time.
13	Forehead	Arch or roll your eyebrows upward. Feel the tension in your forehead. Now, roll your eyebrows back down. Feel your forehead become smooth and relaxed. Repeat 1 more time.
14	Right foot	Slightly lift your foot off the floor. Point your foot and toe. Feel the tension in your calf and leg. Hold it for a moment. Then, release the tension as you return your foot to the floor. Feel your foot and leg relaxing. Repeat 1 more time.
15	Left foot	Do Step 14 for your left foot.
16	Your entire body	Feel your entire body relax. Now, feel it become more deeply relaxed by slowly saying, "My body is more and more relaxed."
17	Breath	Take a deep breath. Breathe deeply as you count from 5 down to 0, with 0 (zero) indicating a very deeply relaxed state. Count down to yourself: "5-4-3-2-1-0."

| 18 | Enjoy | Stay in this relaxed state as long as you desire. We recommend the exercise taking a total of 15 to 20 minutes to obtain the fullest benefit. |

NOTE: When you want to leave your relaxation state, just reverse the count from above. Count from zero up to to five, feeling yourself more awake with each number. Finally, when you get to five, you will feel fully awake and alert. Then, say to yourself, "My relaxation made my body feel lighter. Now, I feel relaxed, refreshed, and fully alert." This helps you feel rested and energized.

Homework: Practice this relaxation technique often. Some people we coached made their own tapes following our step-by-step instructions. Then, they regularly use their tapes. We recommend you do this, too.

Technique #3: Visualization

We have taught people to use visualization techniques to help
- recover or heal from an illness
- control their thoughts and emotions so they can lower their chances of developing illnesses or making them worse

First, let's look at the research conducted on these methods to understand their effectiveness. Research studies have shown the positive effects of visualization on both emotions and health. For example, researchers found a decrease in depression and distress with individuals using a guided imagery (a type of visualization method) and music therapy approach.[3] Additionally, researchers discovered that using visualization combined with music resulted in significant reductions in depression and arthritis.[4] Still other studies found visualization with music decreased the level of depression in research subjects.[5]

A groundbreaking study using guided imagery (a type of visualization) and music found significant decreases in upset moods. In this well-constructed study, research subjects completed questionnaires and had their blood tested for cortisol, a type of stress hormone. Subjects were surveyed before and after using visualization techniques that included music. The researchers found that subjects displayed decreases in negative feelings, depressed mood, and physical fatigue. Importantly, these wonderful benefits remained for at least seven weeks following the study.[6]

Consequently, based on multiple research findings and our Intensive Coaching[SM] expertise, we suggest you combine relaxation, visualization, and music. We especially recommend you use classical music. The combination of classical music in relaxation and visualization has been documented as quite effective.[7, 8, 9]

You may wish to use these classical music suggestions which are verified as effective in research studies on visualization and guided imagery:[10, 11]

- *Introduction and Allegro* by Ravel
- *Pines of Rome* by Respighi
- *Sirenes* from *Nocturnes* by Debussy
- *Passacaglia and Fugue in C Minor* by Bach
- *Little Fugue in G Minor* by Bach
- *Allegro Non Troppo* by Brahms

Our favorite classical music we use is *Canon in D* by Pachelbel. All in all, we highly recommend you turn on classical music when you do your visualization exercises.

How To Use Visualization

As your learned in the relaxation technique, close your eyes and relax. Play classical music in the background, as we suggested. Once relaxed, picture or visualize a time when you sat and relaxed in the sun. Imagine and feel the warmth of the sun on your body. As you feel that warm sensation, direct it to the part of your body that feels sick, injured, or sore.

For example, if you have a sore muscle, direct the warm sensation to your sore muscle. Imagine the sun warming that muscle. Feel the sensation of warmth on your aching muscle. Now, hold onto that sensation as you visualize the soreness in your muscle melting away just like an ice cube melting in the sun. Continue this visualization and warm sensation until all your soreness melts away.

You can customize this visualization technique for your aches or illnessses. For instance, clients we work with have used visualization directed toward healing a variety of ailments, including infections and injuries.

As you use visualization, you may see colors. What might these colors mean? Maryann examined this question in research on visualization, biofeedback, and relaxation.[12] Information on research subjects' emotional states was obtained using sentence completion tests and self-reports. Maryann and psychologist J.S. Martindale, Ph.D., correlated the subjects' emotional states to the colors the subjects reported seeing while doing vizualizations, biofeedback, and relaxation.

You can review the following table to understand what colors you see while visualizing may mean. This could also give you insights into emotions you are experiencing.

Color You See	What's on Your Mind
Bright, clear, green	Healing
Violet	Creativity, spirituality
Orange	Pride
Yellow	Intelligence, power, optimism
Bright red	High-energy or anger
Dark red	Sensuality, sexiness
Dull green	Jeolousy, envy
Black	Dislike, hatred
Dark gray	Pessimism, depression
Blue	Spirituality, calmness

Here are some health-related observations that Maryann and Dr. Martindale noted. On the healthy side, bright clear green seems to be a healing color. In contrast, seeing gray or colors that look dirty and grainy may indicate physical ailments. These ailments could include exhaustion or a developing illness.

Homework: In this chapter, you read about three ways to harness your mind's power to improve your health:
1. Affirmations
2. Relaxation
3. Visualization with classical music

Choose a specific aspect of your health that you desire to improve. For the next week, use these techniques. Experiment to discover which methods prove most useful to you. See for yourself how you can live better using these focused methods. Remember: You need to release any physical anchors that may hold you back from creating and living an optimistic life.

In the next chapter, we will delve into some fairly common yet often misdiagnosed — or even undiagnosed — physical ailments that may be throwing your optimism for a loop.

12

Undiagnosed & Misdiagnosed Illnesses That Smash Your Optimism:

Overcome Common Hidden Illnesses That Drag You Down

In conducting Intensive Coaching^{SM} sessions, we found some individuals had physical ailments that greatly drag down their moods. However, these physical problems often were hidden, misdiagnosed, or even undiagnosed. To help, we did a lot of investigating. We discovered healthcare professionals who understood these ailments. The two most common hidden illnesses encountered were

- light deprivation
- candida

"SAD" from Light Deprivation

Some people experience Seasonal Affective Disorder or SAD when they do not get enough sunlight or natural light. This occurs, because sunlight (or lack of sunlight) affects our
- ◆ physical health
- ◆ moods and emotions

What are the links among sunlight, health, and emotions? Researcher John Ott explains in his book *Health & Light* that human beings are photobiotic and need full-spectrum light or natural sunlight to be healthy.[1]

Sunlight helps energize and regulate your body chemistry. This occurs, because your eyes work somewhat like a plant's photocells. Eyes collect and convert light and its energy into electrical impulses. These electrical impulses are called photocurrents. They flow via the optic nerve to your brain. This photocurrent in the brain (or brain voltage) flows to all your nerves which, in turn, control many bodily functions. So, if you lack exposure to light, such deprivation can throw off your body's natural balance.

Health problems may begin with exposure to florescent or artificial lights. Such lights produce only a narrow color spectrum or energy wavelength. This greatly differs from the full-spectrum light provided by the sun. Health problems also stem from limited exposure to sunlight for people who stay inside a lot.

Studies show that limited-spectrum or typical artificial lights can be harmful to health, according to Dr. Ott. Routinely working in artificially lit environments, such as an office with florescent lights, can deprive people of the proper amount of full-spectrum light needed to maintain healthy bodies.

Optometrist Jacob Liberman, O.D., Ph.D., reports in *Light: Medicine of the Future* that our bodies are living photocells energized by the sun's light. In effect, sunlight is like a nutrient.[2] Dr. Liberman asserts that light profoundly affects our physiological activities and moods. Just as plants need sunlight to nourish and grow, so do humans.

Studies show a connection between light and health. For example, physician Zane Kime, M.D., in his book *Sunlight*, reports that exposure to sunlight produces a metabolic effect in the body similar to that of physical training.[3] For instance, exposure to sunlight helps produce the following:

- decreased resting heart rate
- lowered breathing rate
- reduced blood pressure
- increased tolerance for stress
- boosted energy

Also, Dr. Fritz Hollwich found there is a reduction of stress hormone levels when people used full-spectrum lights.[4] John Ott reports in *Health & Light* and *Light Radiation & You* that on-going research is demontrating how light even helps with immune-deficiency ailments.[5, 6] In fact, he found that red cells in human blood clump into unnatural, long chains and become oxygen-depleted after exposure to the artificial light of video display terminals. Fortunately, using video display terminals in conjunction with full-spectrum lights helps correct this problem. The unnatural chains of red cells were corrected. Also, a healthy flow of oxygen to the cells was restored.

All in all, studies show that lights similiar to natural sunlight may help humans increase energy and alertness, reduce fatigue, regulate sleep-wake cycles, and elevate moods.[7, 8]

Additionally, the amount of sunlight and natural-type light a person gets also affects emotions. For instance, some people feel less energy and sadder moods during winter than during summer. The short days or lack of sunlight leaves some people light-deprived and feeling blue. It is estimated that about 25 million North Americans feel light-deprived.[9, 10]

Optometrist Jacob Liberman explains how this phemonenon of feeling light-starved works. He asserts that the brain's pineal body acts like a type of light meter. This measures the intensity and quality of light. It also acts like a biological clock that measures the brain's exposure to natural light. The brain functions like a solar-powered battery. It, in effect, runs down when we do not get enough light. The solution is to recharge the brain's solar battery with sunlight or natural types of light.

How can you decide if you might be light-deprived? Here are signs to watch for during winter:

◆ decreased mood, such as sadness
◆ low energy
◆ increased consumption of food and food cravings
◆ sleep disturbances
◆ low sex drive
◆ poor concentration

This set of symptoms is called *Seasonal Affective Disorder* or SAD. These symptoms make it difficult to move ahead toward living an optimistic life.

Given this SAD situation, what can you do to overcome such body and mind zappers? The initial solution is to use light therapy.

Light therapy is the daily use of full-spectrum light bulbs or light boxes (similar to sunlight) to replace a lack of sunlight. This lack of sunlight may be due to constantly being inside or the short days of winter. Light therapy has been found to have an antidepressant effect on more than 80 percent of individuals who experience SAD. [11, 12]

A person's mood can change for the better by using light treatment. It has been found to

◆ increase energy
◆ enhance moods
◆ improve sleep cycles

◆ decrease food cravings
◆ increase productivity by improving energy and alertness

The common thread in treating the physical and emotional effects of light deprivation is exposure to sunlight or other full-spectrum light bulbs. As mentioned earlier, full-spectrum lights provide light similar to sunlight.

Here is a list of suggestions you can do to help recharge yourself:

1. *Check your reactions to light deprivation.* Reflect on how you react to overcast days or long winters nights. This helps you determine if you suffer from SAD. If you do, you can try the two suggestions that follow. Also, we recommend you read the books mentioned in this section on light deprivation and SAD.

2. *Use a full-spectrum light.** Most individuals stay inside quite a lot. So, replace your home or office light bulbs with full-spectrum bulbs. For instance, we use these bulbs plus a full-spectrum box-light. Doing so produces wonderful effects, especially during winters.

3. *Walk or sit outside during daylight.* Do this for at least a few minutes everyday. Let the sunlight recharge you.

Candida or Yeast Infections

Candida or yeast infections can really throw your body and mind for a loop. Many healthcare professionals fail to properly diagnose or treat people with candida. They often do not realize that a person with various health problems may be suffering from candida.

---

* To obtain full-spectrum light bulbs or light boxes, see the "Materials You Can Order" section in the back of this book.

What is candida? Candida is a one-celled yeast organism that lives inside every body. It co-exists with good, healthy organisms. Our bodies and immune system usually keep candida cells under control. But sometimes candida gets out of control, multiplies quickly, and produces an array of health problems.

Most people only think of a vaginal infection when they hear about candida. But candida can occur in both men and women in many body parts. It can contribute to many miserable symptoms, including premenstrual syndrome or PMS, reports nutritionist Linaya Hahn in her highly practical book, *PMS: Solving the Puzzle*.[13]

How do people develop sickness-producing yeast imbalances? Physician William Crook, M.D., explains in his book *The Yeast Connection: A Medical Breakthough* that one culprit is overuse of antibiotics.[14] Antibiotics kill both enemy and friendly bacteria. When friendly germs are knocked out, yeast cells or candida multiply quickly. Over time, such growth can weaken a person's immune system. When your immume sytem weakens you may develop

- allergies
- suspectability to infections
- sinus, nose, ear and throat infections
- a constant tired feeling
- poor concentration and memory
- lack of coordination or accident proness
- muscle aches for no apparent reason
- digestive problems
- abdominal pain
- bloating, including a bulging stomach
- repeated colds or flu
- PMS
- irritability

Fortunately, treatment is fairly simple, according to both Dr. Crook and Linaya Hahn. Treatment often includes the following:

1. *Avoid overuse of antibiotics.* Many people gulp down antibiotics as a be-all-and-end-all cure for everything that ails them. Antibiotics kill bacteria, not viruses. However, 80-90 percent of infections are caused by viruses which antibiotics cannot destroy, reports Dr. Crook.[15] So, remember that taking antibiotics may ignite a yeast infection in your body.

2. *Avoid extended uses of "The Pill."* According to Dr. Crook and nutritionist Linaya Hahn, birth control pills may contribute to the development of candida. The birth control pill and its hormones can cause yeast to multiply as vaginitis and other ailments. As such, some women may need to avoid extended uses of birth control pills to help overcome chronic candida.[16]

3. *Carefully choose which foods you eat.* Altering your diet also could help control candida growth. Typical diet changes to help control candida include

◆ avoiding sugar, since sugar feeds candida and helps it multiply
◆ staying away from foods you are allergic to
◆ avoiding yeast, as in bread, since yeast in food could promote the bad yeast growth of candida
◆ taking supplments like acidophilus which could help restore your body's healthy balance

For more details and suggestions on diagnosing and treating candida, you can study the following books:

1. *PMS: Solving the Puzzle* by Linaya Hahn
2. *The Yeast Connection: A Medical Breakthrough* by William Crook, M.D.

Case Example of Successfully Treating Candida

One woman who came to us for Intensive Coaching^SM told us she was constantly getting sick. That hindered her from living much of an active life. This person always felt so drained from her repeated ailments that she had little energy to spare. She would lie on her couch almost every evening feeling horribly fatigued.

Also, she avoided friends and family members, because she felt too ashamed to tell them she was "sick again." As such, she became increasingly isolated and downhearted. And that was not all. Her muscles often felt sore, plus her stomach was constantly bloated and puffed out.

When she developed sinus infections, her physican often prescribed strong antibiotics. One particularly bad sinus infection resulted in a severe ear infection that proved incredibly hard to get rid of.

Finally, tired of her physician's same old advice and the antibiotics sucking out all the energy she had, she reached out to us. Upon hearing her symptoms, we readily suspected this women had candida. We immediately referred her to a healthcare professional (not a physician) who is quite familiar with diagnosing and treating candida. This specialist confirmed that this woman had a bad case of candida.

Eager to feel better, our patient followed every suggestion to the letter. For example, she changed her diet; stopped taking birth control pills and antibiotics; and took special nutritional supplements. She soon began to feel relief.

After a few weeks, she cheerfully exclaimed, "I feel like I had been crawling on the floor, and now I can stand-up and walk. I feel like my batteries are recharging!"

She began to think clearly again and feel energetic. Her health dramatically improved. In Intensive Coaching^SM sessions with us, she joyfully dived into devising and working on her vision and goals. This formerly fatigued, sick and depressed person took control of her life only after she rid her body of candida. She became delightfully healthier, happier, and more optimistic.

Recently, she called us and remarked, "I feel vibrant!!" Her social life has greatly improved. Importantly, she was spending time working on her exciting vision and goals, rather than lying almost lifeless on her couch, suffering from candida.

Homework: Review the information on SAD and candida in this chapter to see if you may be suffering from these often undiagnosed or misdiagnosed ailments. We cited many books in this chapter to help you.

If you have SAD or candida, start doing something about it now. As you remove such physical roadblocks, you will have more energy and time to build health, prosperity and happiness into your life.

Health and wealth create beauty.

ENGLISH PROVERB

13

Ways To Increase Your Prosperity

Affluent people may not be significantly happier than people of more moderate financial means. However, consider these facts:

◆ Much worry is about financial concerns, especially lack of adequate amounts of money.

◆ Many marital spats center on money, especially disagreements about saving, spending, and "not having enough money."

◆ Out of 168 hours/week, most adults spend 40 or more hours working to make money.

Importantly, as reported in their brilliant book *The Millionaire Next Door*, researchers Thomas J. Stanley, Ph.D., and Williams D. Danko, Ph.D., studied millionaires, especially self-made millionaires. These are not trust-fund babies or people who inherited wealth. Their parents did not put silver spoons in their mouths and zillions of dollars in their bank accounts. Instead, Stanley and Danko focus mainly on *self-made* millionaires.

One especially revealing finding zooms in on the optimism question. They divide people into two groups:

◆ Prodigious Accumulators of Wealth (PAWS)
◆ Under-Accumulators of Wealth (UAWS)

Importantly, they found that PAWS tend to have fewer worries than UAWS.[1]

Certainly pessimism — the opposite of optimism — lies at the base of worrying. So, we infer that PAWS worry less and, thus, may well feel more optimistic. In contrast, UAWS would tend to be more pessimistic and less optimistic.

Sometimes when we mention such findings in workshops or speeches we deliver, someone raises his or her hand and makes a cynical comment like, "But, money can't buy happiness!" That is true. No one can purchase happiness. But, everyone knows

◆ Not having enough money certainly can leave you feeling insecure, worried, and unhappy
◆ Accumulating a level of prosperity can help you feel more secure, less worried, proud, and confident. You feel more in-control, which is a hallmark of optimism.

If there is wealth, there is joy.

PHILIPPINE PROVERB

In this chapter, we will not tell you the be-all-and-end-all of achieving prosperity. Instead, we aim to give you concise and to-the-point methods you *easily* can use to achieve

greater financial security. Toward that target, you will find strategies you readily can start using today, including tips on how you can

- save more
- invest easily and wisely
- turn any child into a millionaire

"There are people who have money and people who are rich."

Coco Chanel

Smart Saving Strategies

A chief characteristic of prosperous people, according to Drs. Stanley and Danko boils down to only one word: *frugality.*[2] For instance, we spoke to a self-made millionaire who started from scratch. One of the most fascinating bits of wisdom he mentioned was this: "The best way to have more and more money in your bank account is to *not* spend the money in your bank account!"

How true! And how incredibly simple.

We also met three retired professional athletes who had earned millions of dollars in their heyday. While athletes, they had been written-up in magazines and newspapers with stunning pictures of their glorious houses, cars, wardrobes, and lifestyles. Yet, after retiring from professional sports, each one confided to us that he was worth under $100,000.

How could people who made many *millions* for years be worth under $100,000? Simple. They failed to save and invest. They lived up to a media-popularized image of wealth: Costly houses, cars, clothes, and many other expenses. They now need to work very hard to save for retirement. It is as though they never earned millions of dollars. They essentially could be just as well off if they burned their huge earnings or just tossed their previously monstrous salaries out a window.

"There are two ways to sufficiency and happiness.
We may either diminish our wants or
augment our means;
either will do — the result is the same.
But if you are wise, you will do both at the same time;
and if you are very wise,
you will do both in such a way as to augment
the general happiness of society."

BENJAMIN FRANKLIN

You can use four main methods to make sure you save money toward your own financial security.

Saving Method #1: Pay Yourself First

This is the easiest way to save: Every time you deposit a check, save 10 percent or more of your earnings. Then, you can use the remainder for expenses. This puts you ahead of most people who first spend their income and then, as an afterthought, perhaps save a little money.

By doing this, you conscientiously make sure you accumulate more financial security month after month, year after year. At the very least, you save money. Even better, wisely invest some money, perhaps using methods described later in this chapter.

Saving Method #2: One Week Cooling-off Period

A fruitful way to waste your hard-earned money is to squander it on things you do not really need. Doing so works every time to erode your net worth.

A great way to avoid this financial problem is to use a *1-Week Cooling-Off Period*. Specifically, when you feel compelled to buy something you really do not need, put off purchasing the item for seven days. Then, seven days later — if you still remember the item! — ask yourself, "Do I really need that item? Will my life and future be noticeably better if I spend my money on that?"

It is amazing how often this simple *1-Week Cooling-off Period* helps you avoid unneccessary expenses. For example, we have an old coffee-maker. We both like drinking de-caf coffee. We admired a spectacular coffee-maker in a catalog. We even examined that coffee-maker in a store. As we looked at it, we thought about how delicious the coffee probably would taste and how beautiful the new coffeemaker would look.

As we oohed-&-ahhed over the coffee-maker, we broke out of our reverie long enough to ask ourselves this question: "Do we really need it? If we spend money on it, will our lives be noticeably more wonderful?" Using the method advocated here, we waited a week before deciding about buying the coffee-maker.

Lo and behold, seven days later, the idea of buying a new coffee-maker seemed totally unnecessary. By cooling-off for one week, we

- ◆ overcame an urge to splurge
- ◆ saved money

So, when you feel "hot" to buy something you really may not need, take a *1-Week Cooling-off Period*. That should help you save hundreds or thousands of dollars every year.

Saving Method #3: Buy The Best

After reading the subtitle above, *Buy The Best*, perhaps you are thinking, "They just suggested I save 10 percent and avoid buying unneeded items. But, now they advocate I buy the best. That seems contradictory!"

Let us explain. What we mean by *Buy The Best* is that when you absolutely must buy something, it often is more frugal in the long-run to buy the best.

Here is an example. When Michael finished his doctoral degree, he barely had any money. Then, his long-time pillow fell apart. He bought a cheap pillow figuring that would keep down expenses. Unfortunately, within three months, the filling in the cheap pillow dramatically shifted. It became futile to use the pillow with even the slightest bit of comfort.

Then, rather than buying another cheap pillow, Michael went to a top-notch department store and bought a good quality pillow. The good quality pillow lasted (and proved comfortable) for over 10 years.

So, which pillow was cheaper — the inexpensive pillow that self-destructed in three months or the more costly pillow that lasted over a decade?

The point is that your thrill in buying a cheap item rapidly vanishes if you need to replace the cheap item with a more expensive — and higher quality — item. For instance, the cheap $6 pillow cost $2/month for the three months it lasted. The good quality, more expensive $30 pillow cost only 25-cents/month over the 10 year period. Plus, it provided over 3,650 nights of sleeping comfort.

Saving Method #4: Get The One Very Best Type of Mortgage.

It has been said that a home owner can have only three types of mortgage loans:

- ◆ fixed rate mortgage loan
- ◆ variable rate mortgage loan
- ◆ no mortgage loan

The best type is no mortgage loan at all. The reason is that mortgages are stacked *heavily* in favor of the lender. For instance, a leading mortgage lender told us that a $1,000 per month mortgage principal and interest results in approximately these payments for many years:

- ◆ $200/month goes toward paying off the principal amount borrowed to buy a house
- ◆ $800/month pays for interest

In a sense, for quite a few years, this typical type of mortgage pays only $1 for the house for each $4 paid in interest to the lender. The key lesson here is to

- ◆ buy a house that requires you to borrow little, if any, money
- ◆ pay off all your mortgage loan as fast as possible

Paying off your mortgage may not be easy. But, in the outcome, you have

- ◆ more money in your pocket
- ◆ spent less money making a lender rich

- ◆ peace of mind that you do not owe the money
- ◆ a house owned by you, not the lender

"Nothing but money is sweeter than honey."

BENJAMIN FRANKLIN

Investing Wisely Made Easy

Now that you know to save 10% or more of your income and avoid unneccesary expenses, how can you make your money grow? This can be rather easy and not take much of your precious time.

The key is to put your investing on auto-pilot using relatively low-risk (although not guaranteed) investment methods.

You probably hear about a wide variety of investment options. You can invest in real estate, gold, art, coins, limited partnerships, and many more. These investments often require specialized expertise and a lot of your time. Some are rather speculative, somewhat like gambling with your hard-earned money.

"There are two times in a man's life
when he should not speculate:
When he cannot afford it, and when he can."

MARK TWAIN

A simple method is to invest for the long-term in the stock market. Over the long-term, stocks rise an average of about 10 percent annually. Also, many stocks pay you dividends quarterly.

What follows are three methods you can use that, over a period of years, historically have produced 10 percent or better returns on invested money.

Investment Method #1: Use *"10-10-10"* Criteria to Wisely Choose Mutual Funds

The easiest way to invest in the stock market is through buying shares in mutual funds. A mutual fund provide you with full-time professional investment managers who
- choose stocks and bonds to invest in
- do all the buying, selling and paperwork for you

Some mutual funds perform better than others. To help stack the odds in your favor, you may want to invest only in mutual funds that meet the *10-10-10* criteria. Specifically, this means investing in one or more mutual funds that have
1. been in existence for *10* years or more

2. had the *same person* managing the mutual fund (making the investment decisions) for at least the last *10* years
3. average annual returns (increases in investment values plus dividends) of *10* percent or more per year for *10* years or more

Following these *10-10-10* criteria enables you to invest in a good quality mutual fund. Actually, in effect, you put your money into the hands of *specific* professional money managers who have led their mutual funds to over 10 years of good investment returns. A manager who has successfully managed the *same* mutual fund for 10 years or more has a track record you can feel fairly confident about. The manager has succeeded in both up and down stock markets.

After you find some mutual funds that meet the *10-10-10* criteria, see if you can sleep comfortably with their investment style. For example, you may detest risking your money. If so, then invest only in mutual funds that register fairly modest annuals gains with only one or two modest annual losses over the last 10 years. You can choose from many such conservatively managed, low-risk mutual funds.

Or, if you feel o.k. with more risk, you could look into funds that are more aggressive. Such mutual funds may have bigger annual gains and losses than conservatively managed funds. You must decide if you can sleep soundly with your money at higher risk.

To illustrate the extreme importance of investing only in mutual funds with the *same* manager in-charge for 10 years or longer, simply look at an eye-opening survey done by *U.S. News & World Report* magazine. *U.S. News* asked 10 mutual fund managers for the names of three mutual funds they would invest in for their own retirement.[3] They could not choose the mutual funds they manage.

Out of the 30 mutual funds chosen (10 managers x 3 funds chosen/manager = 30), 16 had been in existence 10 years or more. Of these 16 mutual funds, 14 were managed by the same manager for 10 years or longer. This survey shows that professional money managers know the bottom line benefits of investing using something akin to the *10-10-10* criteria for selecting mutual funds.

You can find information on mutual funds from an array of readily available sources. These include:

◆ Magazines that periodically publish mutual fund investment information, such as *Forbes, Fortune, Money, Mutual Funds, Smart Money, U.S. News & World Report,* & *Worth*
◆ Library
◆ Internet
◆ Mutual fund rating services, such as *Morningstar*

Remember: Pay special attention to mutual funds that meet or exceed the *10-10-10* criteria.

Investment Method #2: Automatic Investment Plan

A key to profitable investing is to invest wisely, long-term, and frequently. Do not expect to make much profit from short-term or speculative investing. Fortunately, investing does not need to take much of your valuable time.

You can use an incredibly easy way to invest monthly — with no extra time or effort on your part. Just sign-up for the monthly "automatic investment plan" when you purchase a mutual fund's shares. You do this on the mutual fund's investment application form.

This enables the mutual fund to automatically take a set amount of money out of your checking account each month and invest it into your mutual fund account. The minimum monthly investment often is just $50/month. To help your money grow faster, you probably want to invest more each month.

Doing so helps you in a few ways. First, your automatic investment plan assures you definitely invest regularly. This is important, because all too often people forget or put off investing their savings.

Second, your monthly automatic investment plan lets you take advantage of dollar-cost averaging. Your monthly investment will buy more shares for you when share prices fall, and less when share prices rise. The outcome: Over the long-term, your average cost per share probably will be lower than if you bought all your shares at only one time.

Third, automatic monthly investing makes you avoid emotional buying and selling of your mutual fund investments. Over long periods of time, stock prices tend to rise. Some years prices fall and in other years they rise. Many people hesitate to buy when stock prices decline. But, this can be a good time to buy mutual fund shares, since sooner or later stock prices will rise, and so should your mutual fund shares' value. Your monthly automatic investments assures you keep investing for the long-term.

Fourth, and most importantly, as you keep investing each month, you move toward financial prosperity. For example, let's say you want to accumulate $1-million in mutual fund investments. According to financial advisor Tod Barnhart, in his book *The Five Rituals of Wealth*, if you earn 12 percent annually on your investments, you need to invest about the these amounts monthly:[4]

Each month you invest...	Then you will have $1-million in...
$4,345	10 years
$2,000	15 years
$1,000	20 years
$535	25 years
$285	30 years
$155	35 years
$85	40 years

For instance, if you want $1-million in 20 years, you need to invest about $1,000 monthly. Pick the deadline by which you want a certain amount of money. Then, use automatic monthly investing to reach your goal.

Always keep this in mind: In the short-term, good mutual funds go up and down in value. But, to your benefit, over the long-term the odds are in your favor. So, your long-term, monthly investing creates real reasons to feel optimistic about your financial future.

Investment Method #3: Buy 5 Specific Dow Jones Industrial Average Stocks

The *Dow 5* investment method resulted in 23.21 percent average annual gains over a recent 15 year period and 21.36 percent average annual gains over a 25 year period.[5, 6] This does not include sales fees, taxes, or commissions. Yet, even after such expenses, the *Dow 5* strategy has been quite profitable over the long haul.

You can use the *Dow 5* investment method quite easily. But remember, you should do this over many years or decades to benefit from this long-term investment strategy.

Specifically, buy the five highest yielding, lowest priced stocks in the Dow Jones Industrial Average (DJIA). The DJIA is the most famous stock market average. It consists of stocks of 30 well-known, large companies, including AT&T, Coca-Cola, DuPont, General Electric, and General Motors. These are well-managed companies that lead their industries.

You can take advantage of this fairly low-risk, long-term way to profit from the DJIA. To do this, you follow these steps:

Step 1: Make a list of the 10 highest yielding DJIA stocks; "yield" is the dividend's percentage of stock price, e.g., a $100/share stock with a $5 dividend has a 5 percent yield.

Step 2:   From these 10 stocks, make a list of the 5 lowest price
            stocks.
Step 3:   Invest the same number of dollars into each of these
            five stocks, e.g., if you invest $5,000 total, then invest
            $1,000 in each of the 5 stocks listed in Step 2.
Step 4:   Keep these stocks for exactly one year.
Step 5:   At the end of one year, do Steps 1-4 again.
Step 6:   Keep doing Steps 1-5 for many years, preferably
            10-20 years.

Perhaps you do not want to spend your time doing Steps
1-6. Fortunately, you can use an even simpler way to benefit
from this *Dow 5* strategy. Most stock brokerage firms offer a
unit investment trust (UIT) which does all the buying, selling, and paperwork for you. Just call a stock brokerage firm
to receive information.

A small percentage of your UIT price goes toward commissions and record-keeping. It seems like a small price to
pay for the peace-of-mind and potential profits of a hassle-
free, long-term, fairly low-risk investing method.

You Can Make Any Child Into A Millionaire

You can turn a child into a millionaire. It is easy, and will cost
you very little money.

Many parents, grandparents, aunts and uncles would
love to give "the perfect gift" to a newborn. Typical gifts are
very touching, but provide only time-limited usefulness, such
as baby clothes or toys. Then, as the child grows, presents
often are even more toys and clothes.

We visited one home in which a seven year-old child
owned over $5,000 of toys! Yet, the child's favorite toy was a
$5 item. The other $4,995 of toys just sat unused — until the
family would recycle or discard them. What a waste!

So, here is an unusual gift you can give that will financially benefit your child, grandchild, niece, or nephew. At his or her birth, give the child $1,000 invested in a good-quality mutual fund; use the *10-10-10* criteria explained earlier in this chapter. If possible, stipulate that the child cannot touch the money for 60 years. For example, some mutual fund companies offer special trust-type mutual funds in which you can specify that a child cannot remove any money until a certain age. If the $1,000 grows at 12 percent annually, then at age 60, that $1,000 will be worth about $1-million! At age 65, the $1,000 would be worth about $1.5-million!!

Of course, inflation and taxes will affect the outcome, too. One woman with whom we conducted Intensive Coaching^{SM} sessions recently became a grandmother. She had spent her entire life raising a family, loving her husband, and working. In retirement with no children to raise, she felt a void about what to do with her life.

She created a Vision Statment that included helping her grandchildren succeed in life. One of her first goals was to invest $1,000 for each of her grandchildren. She also gave them toys and, especially, loads of love and attention.

She called us six years after her Intensive Coaching^{SM} sessions. She told us, "Almost all the toys I gave my grandchildren are doing nothing, except collecting dust. But the $1,000 I invested for each of them is growing, and it will make a world of difference for them."

If you would feel happy helping a child achieve financial security, perhaps a $1,000 mutual fund investment is better than $1,000 of toys. The child's interest in a toy you give him or her usually lasts one minute to a few months. The value of your $1,000 investment can make a long-term difference in that special child's life.

Prosperity is the fruit of industry,
while idleness begets proverty.

AUSTRALIAN PROVERB

Of course, money is not the only legacy you want to leave. You also want to help children develop optimistic lives. And the next chapter reveals how you can succeed at doing that.

14

You Can Help
Other People Become
Optimistic – –
Including Your Children

Hundreds of our workshop participants and Intensive Coaching[SM] clients made this sort of request to us: "Optimism methods you showed us work great and improved my life. How can I help other people I love and care about — children, spouse, family, friends, and co-workers — become more optimistic, too?" This chapter shows you how. Importantly, many of our workshop participants and clients told us they especially want to raise optimistic children. So, the final section of this chapter guides you in how to raise your children to be optimists.

Here Is Exactly How A Person Becomes A Pessimist or An Optimist

One day as we walked down a street, we observed how

people learn to become pessimistic or optimistic. A little child was running incredibly fast. All of a sudden he fell down so hard that we thought he would break the concrete sidewalk!

As he picked himself up, his mother rushed to his side and frantically screamed, "Oh, my little darling, are you o.k.? Where are you bleeding? I bet you hurt horribly! Where do you hurt? Are you o.k.? You must be horribly hurt!!"

Just then, the mother burst into tears. One-half second later, her child also burst into tears.

A few minutes later, we saw another little child running incredibly fast down the same sidewalk. All of a sudden, this child fell really hard.

The child picked himself up, looking a bit dazed from the hard blow. His mother ran up to him and exclaimed, "Oh, my little darling, are you o.k.? You're such a good kid. You fell down, but I bet you're fine. I'm so proud of you! Let me kiss you."

Just then, the mother smiled. One moment later, her child started smiling and laughing. The mother hugged and kissed her child.

Can you guess which child will grow up pessimistic and depressed? And can you predict which child will grow up optimistic, happy, and confident?

We heard a marvelous phrase: *It's never too late to have a happy childhood.*

Of course, you cannot go back in time to make sure your parents acted like the second mother in the story you just read. But, as you learned so far in this book, you definitely can transform yourself into an optimistic, confident individual.

Now, let's turn to a glorious ability you possess, even if you do not realize it yet. You possess the ability to help other people become dramatically more optimistic. You can do this with people you love and deeply care about, including your children and spouse. Also, you can lead the way to your co-workers developing greater optimism.

Your Powerful Influence on Others: Be An Optimistic Role Model

You help people develop greater optimism when you are a superb role model who oozes optimism. Doing so requires you to use methods you read about earlier in this book, including

♦ 60-second tips to instantly feel optimistic
♦ Positive Mind Conditioning™

First, teach others through your own example the *key to Positive Mind Conditioning™: You can have only one thought at a time in your mind.* Most importantly,

♦ Spread the word on this powerful, yet seldom learned, key to optimism
♦ Let people see you focusing your "one thought at a time" on positive thoughts and feelings, especially on your inspiring vision and goals

When your children, spouse, co-workers, friends and others see you dwelling on positive items, they get a clear picture of how they can do likewise.

Second, *exude upbeat attitudes.* You can do this in a number of ways. Most important of all, constantly do the following: *Focus on solutions, not problems. Avoid complaining.* After all, pessimistic and depressed people dwell on complaining and unearthing problems. Optimistic, happy and healthy people focus on conjuring up solutions and implementing them. Remember:

*Attitudes can be contagious.
Are your attitudes really worth catching?*

Other upbeat attitudes you need to exhibit in your everyday actions include you

◆ *Expecting the best*
◆ *Showing strong ambition* to achieve your vision and goals
◆ *Using flexible thinking*, including admitting when you are wrong or changing your mind when you discover better ways to do things
◆ *Demonstrating persistence* by plugging away until you complete each project you start

Third, *use upbeat words*. To do this, replace words with negative connotations with words that evoke neutral or positive moods. For example, do not let your children, spouse, friends or co-workers hear you say negative words like "nervous," "overwhelmed," or "hyper." Instead, use more positive words in their place, such as "concerned," "challenged," or "alert." Also, make sure you

◆ praise often
◆ reward other's successes
◆ tactfully correct or critize their shortcomings

Fourth, *act cheerful*. Remember: You *feel* whatever emotion you are *acting* at the moment. This is a crucial tenet of psychology. For instance, to be an optimistic role model, you want to consistently act optimistic.

The easiest way to act cheerful is to *use a cheerful tone of voice*. Doing this is quick, does not cost you a penny, and you feel good. Plus, your cheerful vocal demeanor makes you a spectacular, easy to emulate role model.

Fifth, *keep your posture straight*. Earlier in this book, we discussed how your posture simultaneously reveals *and* reinforces your mood. For instance, depressed or pessimistic people tend to slouch their heads and shoulders. They often walk in small steps.

In contrast, optimistic and upbeat people use straight posture. They keep their heads back and high, shoulders back, chest out, and take somewhat longer and more confident steps. When you use straight posture, you physically exude optimism. That, too, benefits your family members, friends, and co-workers.

5 Consistent Actions of An Optimistic Role Model

Being a superb, optimistic role model is mighty uncomplicated. It boils down to you always using five key actions. We distilled these vital actions from our research, personal trial-&-error, plus feedback from clients who went through our Intensive Coaching^SM sessions. To be an optimistic role model, consistently do the following five actions.

Action #1: You Make Relationships Fun

Many psychologists, psychiatrists and family therapists *incorrectly* say that the most important component of a relationship is "communication." That is wrong! It misses the mark!! As you know, a lot of awful relationships include tons of "communication." It is awful, destructive "communication." So, "communication" is not the key.

Instead, we repeatedly find spectacular, healthy relationships possess one key ingredient: *FUN*. Think about it for a moment. Probably, all your most delightful, cherished family, friendship and work relations include having fun with those people. As we like to say:

"When the fun goes out, the sun goes out!"

MICHAEL W. MERCER & MARYANN V. TROIANI

So, your first action as an optimistic role model is to inject *fun* into relating with your children, spouse, and co-workers.

Action #2: You Are A Cheerleader

Imagine a person who helps you feel wonderful about your successes. That person acts as your cheerleader. You savor the fuss your cheerleader makes over you.

As a role model, you need to act like a cheerleader. How do you do that? Praise their successes. Their big successes earn your praise. Even their little successes elicit praise from you. Importantly, praise helps instill optimism in others when your praise is

- ◆ for *real* achievements
- ◆ frequent
- ◆ immediate
- ◆ given with direct eye-to-eye contact
- ◆ accompanied by *appropriate* physical contact, such as a "pat on the back," hugs, kisses, or handshakes

*"We can't all be heroes,
because someone has to sit on the curb
and clap as they go by."*

WILL ROGERS

Action #3: You Show Empathy — Not Sympathy — for Their Feelings

People love and need to have their emotions listened to and understood. Superb role models do this with empathy, not sympathy. Empathy means you show that you understand their feelings, moods, and reactions.

Do not use sympathy. Doing so means you would get entangled in their emotional webs and experience their same feelings. Little children show sympathy, for example, when they cry while they watch another person cry. In contrast, mature adults and useful role models tend to empathize, not sympathize. So, when your child, spouse or co-worker feels a negative emotion, you provide a great role model when you do the following: Show you *understand* and care about their pain, but do not *feel* their pain.

Action #4: You Focus on Solutions, Not Complaining

Optimists solve while pessimists complain. As a role model, use this fact of optimistic life. Do not complain. Instead, you need to show them that you constantly focus on turning problems into solutions and opportunities. Importantly, praise or reward your family members, friends and co-workers each time they

- ◆ conjure up a solution
- ◆ put a solution into action

"I praise loudly. I blame softly."

CATHERINE THE GREAT

One great way to subtly teach someone to focus on solutions is this: Every time the person complains, say something like, "I understand that certainly seems like a challenge. What solutions could help you?"

If the person pouts and groans, "I don't know," remain unfazed. Then immediately ask, "Well, what do you imagine might be a good solution?" Then, calmly let them talk through their ideas. Praise them as they think up solutions.

The point is that you provide a real, live example of a cheerful person who expects them to come out on top. Eventually, your confidence in them will become contagious. They will catch it from you.

Action #5: You Tactfully Correct A Person Using The "CAP" Method

Just because you want to be a fun, praising, empathic, solution-focused role model does not mean you avoid correcting people or telling them they are wrong. They key is to put this proverb into action:

*A car can go just as far on square wheels
as it can go on round wheels.
The difference is that on round wheels
the ride is much smoother.*

FRENCH PROVERB

Correct people diplomatically (using "round wheels"), not by hitting them between the eyes (using "square wheels") with stinging criticism.

Key point to remember: *Focus on their incorrect or not useful action or behavior. Do not attribute their missteps to a personality or mental flaw.* For instance, you might say, "It did not work out when you did X, Y, and Z actions." Do not say, "You proved too lazy (personality flaw) and dumb (mental flaw) to do that."

Also, implore the person to come up with solutions or improved ways to do things. Finally, praise their feasible solutions. We call this the 3-step *CAP* method:

Step 1: Comment on the person's actions, not personality or brainpower. Example: "It did not work well when you did X, Y, and Z."

Step 2: Ask the person for possible solutions. Example: "How could you handle that next time?"

Step 3: Praise reasonable solutions the person tells you. Example: "You came up with a fantastic solution!"

*"Correction does much,
but encouragement does more."*

GOETHE

Raising Optimistic Children

Importance of Turning Your Children into Optimists

One of the most profound influences a parent can exert is to help a child become optimistic. After all, an upbeat approach to living helps a child develop into a healthy, prosperous and happy adult. Aren't those objectives every parent desires for his or her offspring?

This section gives parents tips to raise optimistic, "Can-Do," confident children. If you are not a parent, you still can use these methods. Apply these techniques with your grand-children, nephews, nieces, students, and other children. You can make a profound difference in their lives.

Most importantly, keep in mind that children "catch" their parents' emotions. For example, University of Washington researchers Carole Hooven, Lynn Katz and John Gottman examined links between parents' emotional maturity and their children's success in everyday life activities.[1] Sure enough, emotionally mature parents raise children who perform better in school in particular and life in general. Those children, compared to children of emotionally imma-ture or unstable parents, do better

- ◆ *Academically* — including higher reading and math scores, even for children with similar IQs

- *Behaviorally* — teachers and parents report the children act more in-control and less pesky
- *Biologically* — lower stress hormone levels
- *Emotionally* — less emotional distress and more ability to handle trying situations
- *Socially* — relate better with people

Such fabulous results point to a guideline you can use in raising your children:

- Emotionally stable parents tend to produce *dream* children
- Emotionally unstable parents are more likely to create *nightmare* children

Since children "catch" their parents emotions, you may well ask how that occurs. University of Pennsylvania psychologist Martin Seligman, Ph.D., says children learn their parents' explanatory style.[2] In general, optimistic parents explain difficulties in such a way that the child learns problems or crises

- can be solved
- only concern the specific difficulty and not a lot of other problems

On the other hand, pessimistic parents employ a much different way to explain difficulties that pop up. Their explanations of problems teach their children that set-backs are

- not fixable
- permanent, forever, and will not change
- going to arise again and again

That is, optimistic parents teach children that everything in life can be handled. In sharp contrast, pessimistic parents, in effect, teach their offspring that the fairy tale character "Chicken Little" was right that "the sky really is falling."

And that is not all. All parents want their children to learn well. Of course, intelligence gives children the ability to learn. Beyond that, optimistic children are more likely to be emotionally ready to absorb material they must learn.

In fact, a report by the National Center for Clinical Infant Programs lists these optimism-related factors that impact a child's readiness to learn:[3]

◆ Confidence — a basic component in optimism
◆ Cooperativeness — an optimistic child is more trusting and, as such, cooperative
◆ Internal locus-of-control — a key trait of optimistic people

All this can start a wonderful, self-perpetuating cycle. First, children "catch" these optimism traits from their parents. Optimism then helps the child do better in school. Both child and parents find this very rewarding. Such academic success rewards the child's belief that he or she has real reasons to feel confident, cooperative, and in-control. The following diagram shows this wheel of success:

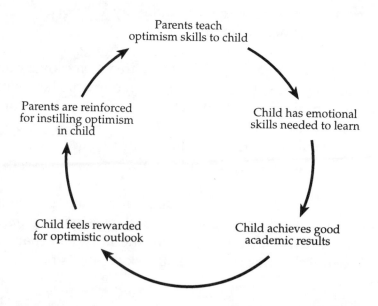

Parents teach
optimism skills to child

Parents are reinforced
for instilling optimism
in child

Child has emotional
skills needed to learn

Child feels rewarded
for optimistic outlook

Child achieves good
academic results

In fact, classic research on high-achievers confirms our observations.[4] Harvard psychologist David McClelland, Ph.D., a distinguished researcher on achievement motivation, found that parents of high-achieving kids exhibit key "Can-Do" qualities. They

◆ are open-minded
◆ expect the best
◆ encourage — and involve themselves in — homework

So, now let's delve into how you can instill optimism in your child.

Instilling Optimism in Your Child

As we promised, now we will show you how to raise optimistic children. To do this, we recommend you use the five actions of an optimistic role model.

Action #1: Have Fun With Your Child

We have appeared as psychologists on many TV talk shows. One show dealt with mother-daughter relationships. It featured six mother and their daughters. Some of them share delightful relationships, while others have frightful relationships.

Before the show, we privately talked with the mothers and daughters. One question we asked was, "What is most striking about your relationship?" That phrase could be taken in either a positive or negative light.

The answers proved incredibly revealing. The mothers and daughters who bicker a lot invariably launched into their myriad disagreements and grudges.

On the other hand, the mothers and daughters who cherish each other *always* blurted out the exact *same* response. They all said the "most striking" ingredient in their relationship is *"Fun."*

During the talk show, the host asked us to give psychological commentary on a number of topics. We pointed out that *"fun"* — and not just "communication" — is the primary trait of each healthy, enjoyable mother-daughter relationship. The lousy mother-daughter pairs had loads of "communication." They consistently communicated discord, disgust and discomfort with each other.

In contrast, each happy mother-daughter pair oozed *fun.* They tremendously enjoyed doing certain activities together. Plus, they tended to focus on their commonalities, not their differences.

Question: Why is having fun a crucial ingredient in raising healthy kids?

Answer: It proves vastly easier to influence your child if your child enjoys being with you. You will have an uphill battle being an optimistic role model if your child considers you a chore to be near.

Homework: Sit down with your child. Make a list of activities *both* you and your child would enjoy doing together. Jointly plan when you can do each activity. Carry out your plan.

"We despise no source that can pay us a pleasing attention."

MARK TWAIN

Action #2: You Are Your Child's Cheerleader

Think back to when you were a child. Remember a time when you came home feeling ultra-proud of something you did. You walked into your home, and proudly announced your big accomplishment. And your parents oohed and ahhed and made a big fuss over how wonderful you were. Maybe they hugged and kissed you, too. You felt on top of the world.

What did your parents do that left you feeling ultra-special?

They acted like *cheerleaders* with you, and you loved it. Children need lots of positive remarks, praise and compliments from their parents. These factors greatly affect their emotional and attitude development.

When you act like your child's cheerleader, you start a magnificent chain reaction. First, your excitement shows you reward accomplishments. Your child receives the between-the-lines message that doing well (in school, activities or relationships) gets attention. In contrast, many pessimistic children feel depressed, because they get dumped on when they fail and ignored when they succeed.

Second, your cheerleading serves as a magnificent example they can follow. Specifically, we discovered:

*"Optimists live to cheer.
Pessimists live to boo."*

Michael W. Mercer & Maryann V. Troiani

Third, when your child feels the warmth and enthusiasm of your cheering, he or she learns how to act. Sooner or later, your child will see another child do something great. Your child will compliment that kid. Then, that kid will like your child more. Children with friends have good reason to feel comfortable interacting. That gives your child even more reason to feel optimistic, confident, and socially adept.

Homework: Conjure up all the ways you could be your child's cheerleader. Then, each time he or she proudly tells you about an accomplishment, act like a cheerleader. Ooh and ahh and drool (verbally) over your child. Kiss, hug, and help your child feel special. Let him or her bask in your glow.

Action #3: Show Your Child Love, Understanding, & Empathy

Perhaps the most important optimistic role modeling you can do is this: Make sure your child knows you feel unconditional love for him or her. This means that you love your child no matter what happens. You may not like some of your child's *actions* or *behaviors*. However, an outstanding parent always loves the child as a *person*.

Here are ways you can make sure your child knows you love him or her. First, *frequently say, "I love you"* to your child. Your voice must convey how much you mean it. Also, make sure your actions say this, too. Next, give your child *uninterrupted attention*. Spend "quality time" together. This includes
- being alone with your child
- listening while they tell you about their activities and feelings
- empathizing with their emotions
- using prolonged, caring eye-to-eye contact; this conveys "I'm with you and you're important to me"

◆ hugging and kissing your child; physical displays of affection give the message that "You're special to me, and I love you."

In fact, a common trait of emotionally disturbed and upset individuals is their feeling that they are not totally loved by at least one person. Their quirky behaviors and uneasy feelings flow from craving attention and love.

Interestingly, Maryann years ago counseled teenagers in a psychiatric hospital. She discovered how this problem consumed many troubled teenagers. Many times an adolescent's unhappiness and depression directly related to feeling unloved or lacking in love from his or her parents. Often, the teenager's annoying acting-out antics were a way to seek attention to help heal their emotional wounds.

Keep in mind that your child will not always be on a non-stop winning streak. Everyone hits bumps and potholes on the road of life. Children hit bumps at home, school, in the neighborhood, with other kids, and more.

At those times, your heart goes out to your child. You wish they did not feel disaappointments, anguish, and heartaches.

To be a optimistic role model, muster up your courage to give empathy, but not sympathy, to your child.

Empathy means I
understand and care *about your pain.*
*Sympathy means I **feel** your pain.*

Optimists empathize. Pessimists tend to sympathize. After all, it is hard to feel optimistic if the chills and spills of someone else's life frays and tatters your feelings.

When your child feels upset, the best prescription is a strong dose of empathy. First, listen carefully to their feelings. People love being listened to.

Second, sensitively put their emotions into words. Labeling emotions is a learned skill. Your children need to learn it from you. Sometimes just labeling an uncomfortable emotion has a healing effect. In fact, a method of psychotherapy called "client-centered therapy" is based on this phenomenon.

For example, you might say something like this: "When that kid did that to you, you felt embarrassed." Your child's upset may lessen just by learning from you that the horrible emotion has a name, "embarrassed."

Action #4:   Show Your Kids You Focus on Solutions, Not Problems

Children learn best by seeing what you do, not by what you tell them to do.

As a role model, a key goal is to help your child "catch" an optimistic way of thinking. A hallmark of optimistic thinking is to focus on solutions, rather than on complaining.

*"Optimists solve.
Pessimists complain."*

MICHAEL W. MERCER & MARYANN V. TROIANI

When you encounter a problem, crisis or set-back, make sure your child sees you

- ◆ immediately snap into a problem-solving mode
- ◆ skip complaining or bemoaning your predicament

An advanced role-modeling method is to ask your child for ideas to solve a problem. This was beautifully illustrated by the child of one of our friends.

We dropped by just as our friend was sweeping the floor with an electric broom. The electric broom suddenly conked out and would not work.

Our friend turned to his child and calmly said, "The electric broom broke. How can we sweep the floor?"

The child pondered the question awhile. Then, a big smile spread across the child's face as she suggested, "Let's use a regular broom." Then, the child ran to a closet, grabbed two brooms and a dustpan, and handed one broom to her father. Then, father and daughter together swept the floor. When they finished, the little problem-solver proudly asked her father, "Do you need my advice on anything else?"

As we mentioned earlier, psychologist David McClelland, Ph.D., is the guru of achievement motivation. He found high-achieving children often come from families that encourage children to problem-solve about family matters. Such shared problem-solving conveys respect to the child. Showering praise on your children for problem-solving (a skill they learn by watching you) leads your child to feeling confident, competent, and optimistic.

"Give a man a fish,
and you feed him for one day.
Teach him how to fish,
and you feed him for a lifetime."

Lao Tzu

Action #5: CAP Correcting Your Child

If self-esteem is like a balloon that floats through the air, then destructive criticism is like a pin that punctures the balloon and makes it splat on the ground.

Destructive criticism is criticizing your child to make him or her feel *like a flawed person*. These flaws may include mental ability, personality, or character flaws. In fact, kids frequently pull off an amazingly horrible feat. After a lot of destructive criticism, children often exhibit the exact intellectual, personality or character flaw contained in their parent's destructive criticism.

*"The tragic truth is that the language of
'victimization' is the true victimizer — a great
crippler of young minds and spirits. To teach
young people that their lives are governed not
by their own actions, but by socioeconomic
forces or government budgets or other
mysterious and fiendish forces beyond their
control, is to teach our children negativism,
resignation, passivity and despair."*

LOUIS W. SULLIVAN

For example, at local gatherings over a period of a few
years, we often saw one mother destructively criticize her
son. She kept calling him "stupid." At one event, we wit-
nessed her calling him "stupid" 25 times before we stopped
counting.

From talking to the boy, we judged he was average or
better in intelligence. We have developed and administered
enough mental abilities tests to detect a person's general level
of intelligence just from talking the person. So, we knew the
boy definitely was not "stupid." We speculated that if his
mother often called him "stupid" in front of other people,
she probably spoke even worse to him in private.

Sure enough, that mother's "stupid" son never finished
school!! His underachieving, in effect, proved his demeaning mother right. This situation is meant to warn you: *Be care-
ful what you tell your child about his or her intelligence and personality, because your child might prove you right.*

Fortunately, we devised a three-step method you can use to correct or positively critique your child. We call it the *CAP Method:*

- ◆ Comment on your child's actions; importantly, do not accuse the child of intellectual or personality imperfections
- ◆ Ask your child to problem-solve how to do better in the future
- ◆ Praise your child for coming up with a viable solution

For example, perhaps your child earned a low grade on an exam. Using the *CAP Method*, you might make these statements:

1. *Comment on the action:* "You earned a `C' on this exam."
2. *Ask for a solution:* "What can you do to earn a better grade on the next exam?"
3. *Praise:* [After hearing child's feasible solution] "That's a great idea!"

The *CAP Method* lets you implement ingredients of optimism. First, by commenting on your child's specific actions, you critique while still showing unconditional love for him or her. Next, you encourage problem-solving, rather than complaining. Finally, you reward or praise your child for being a resourceful problem-solver. Best of all, you improve your child's self-esteem and your relationship with your child.

Homework: The next 10 times your child does something you want to correct or critique, calmly use the *CAP Method.* This takes practice. Importantly, notice how your child likes problem-solving and receiving praise. The results are worth it for your child — and for you as a role-model of optimism.

15

Interviews With Optimistic, Highly Successful People

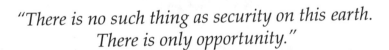

"There is no such thing as security on this earth.
There is only opportunity."

DOUGLAS MACARTHUR

In the previous chapters, you learned techniques, principles and research to help you become an optimist. To help you further, we interviewed optimistic yet "ordinary" people who have achieved tremendous success. We purposely did not include anyone who is a monstrous, front-page, headline-grabber. Why? Because that would not prove helpful to most people.

Instead, we interviewed five individuals and one couple who built their lives from scratch using optimism and hard work. Their successes provide you with magnificent role models to help you in your quests. Importantly, you will see how these wonderful people exhibit our principles of optimism you learned in this book.

To conduct the interviews, we asked each one the same 10 questions. As you read their stories, you will notice how their confident, "Can-Do" attitudes combined with their hard work, persistence and strong belief in their exciting visions to create absolutely fabulous lives.

We are sure you will benefit from reading their real-life stories.

Building *Success* Magazine & A Whole Lot More:

Scott DeGarmo

When we decided to include interviews with optimistic, successful people in our book, we drew up a list of people who would benefit our readers. At the top of our list was Scott DeGarmo. He has spent 13 years serving as editor and publisher of *Success* magazine. Our interview of Scott proved quite exciting for us. As chief of *Success* magazine, he learned first-hand what incredibly successful people do. Importantly, Scott puts these insights into action in both his personal and business life.

Success magazine was around for decades when Scott arrived at the publication. However, it did not have a clearly pinpointed readership or "demographic" that potential subscribers or advertisers could readily identify. Scott set out to correct that.

His exciting vision for *Success* magazine was the following: "Help entrepreneurs find a way to understand and master the entrepreneurial process, and bring them vital information that would help them."

You can see Scott's vision is *big*. His vision was to help the people who vastly improve the lives of millions of people through their services, products, innovation, and employment opportunities. As you learned in this book, visions work best when they are big and include helping other people improve their lives. Scott's vision certainly fits this gauge.

How has he done in achieving his vision? Scott's results are astounding. Over a 13 year period, he led *Success* magazine from 200,000 circulation to a 1.6-million readership! This is even more amazing when you consider that Scott has been one of the few executives of a major periodical to simultaneously be both

- editor-in-chief (in charge of written content)
- publisher (head of the magazine's business)

To achieve such spectacular results, Scott told us he started with four main goals:

- Beat newsstand sales of a competing magazine "by two to one — and we exceeded that"
- "Establish a listing for graduate schools that teach entrepreneurship"
- "Have the most successful yearly series on raising capital"
- "I especially wanted to hear individual stories by people who were helped by *Success* magazine. Their letters and calls are what really motivated me."

Speaking with Scott, we were impressed with how much his optimism fuels his career and personal success. Scott explained,

> *Optimism helps me see possibilities that otherwise would not be apparent. It gives me the toughness and resolve to keep going when the path gets difficult. Also, optimism gives me excitement about my goals and mission to help draw other people to me.*

We also felt quite touched by how Scott injects optimism in his personal life. For example, he described, "Going on a family outing with an optimistic outlook helps assure we'll have a good time." This surely seems like a delightful way to approach family activities.

Scott also realizes his optimism enables him to serve as a healthy role model for his children. From him, they learn "an optimistic outlook in what they do. It's everything from getting up in the morning to the spirit in which I approach the tasks in my life." Earlier, you read a chapter on how to be an optimistic role model. The way Scott handles family matters with a confident, "Can-Do," upbeat manner helps assure a great family life plus the opportunity to raise optimistic children.

His attitudes also reflect on Scott's optimistic strategy. He told us four key attitudes stand out as especially helpful. You will recognize Scott's attitudes as characteristic of attitudes held by optimistic people who make things happen in their lives:

- ◆ "Persistence and drive"
- ◆ "Belief that I will be able to turn things to my advantage and make things work out"
- ◆ "I'm responsible for my outcomes. I take control of my life."
- ◆ "Take joy and pleasure from what I'm doing."

Also, Scott frequently says to himself certain phrases or affirmations that help him focus on what he considers most important. These include the following:

- "I'm in charge of my life."
- "I'm immunized against depression, disappointments, disease, and other negative influences"
- "I'm ready to seize opportunities."
- Before going to bed, Scott programs his mind by saying,
    "I will awaken with positive thoughts and emotions and with creative solutions to the problems before me."
    "When I get up, I'll get up with an energetic and enthusiastic outlook."
- "I keep my important goals in front of me in writing and repeat them every day, stoking my white hot desire for achievement."
- "I visualize my goals with clarity."
- "I vividly envision, feel and taste future outcomes while keeping my attention focused on present actions."

Imagine saturating your mind with affirmations and phrases like Scott's. Doing so would program you to keep sharply focused on what you most want in your life. If you like, you can regard Scott as an energetic role model for his powerful — and obviously helpful — affirmations.

Which brings us to the subject of whom Scott considers his role models. He mentioned three. First, Thomas Alva Edison, the inventor of the electric light bulb, motion pictures, and founder of the company we now know as General Electric. From studying Edison, Scott learned, "Enormous persistence. Edison never looked at things as failures or setbacks. He just looked at them as a chance to try again. For example, when it took Edison a very long time to find the right filament for the light bulb, he just kept looking until he found it."

Second, Scott admires Leeuwenhoek, the Dutchman who invented the microscope. Leeuwenhoek's lesson for Scott is the value of "complete, total involvement in his work. He was an uneducated man who became a member of the prestigious Royal Academy of Sciences."

Finally, Scott's third role model is Theodore Roosevelt. Scott explains, "He invented himself. He was an asthmatic, frail child. But, he built himself up through physical effort to become a great horseman, boxer, soldier, and statesman. The fact he started as such a puny physical specimen is what's impressive about him."

Scott does not personally know his three role models. You, too, do not need to actually meet your role models. Just find people who strike a chord in you. Read about them in books and articles. Like Scott did, discover the lessons you find valuable from each role model. Then, adopt or adapt your role model's methods to help you effectively handle situations.

As such a dynamic person, Scott is not about to rest on his laurels. After his spectacular success with *Success* magazine, what is Scott's exciting vision for his future? Scott enthusiastically told us, "I'm going to create a publishing venture that takes entrepreneurial education to a new level. It'll go beyond what I did in the past."

You learned earlier in this book that once you achieve your exciting vision, create another exciting vision and go for it. Scott DeGarmo is a magnificent example of someone doing that. From chatting with Scott, we feel certain he will achieve whatever he focuses on doing — *again*. After all, using optimism and hard work, Scott has made a habit out of success.

Busting Beauty Industry Myths:

Robert Holdheim & Shafi Saxena

When we spoke with Robert Holdheim and Shafi Saxena, founders of Better Botanicals, we felt awed by their extremely passionate belief in their unique products, along with their marketing savvy. Their store in Washington, D.C., mail order business and busy Web site offer natural, aromatherapeutic, herbal products for skin, hair, bath and body care. Unlike most skin care items, their products come in *real* glass containers and contain no artificial colors, fragrances, mineral oils, or harsh chemicals. In other words, what you see *is* what you get. This differs greatly from typical skin care products made of who-knows-what-and-you-may-not-want-to-find-out!

Their exciting vision is to "bust a few beauty industry myths and bring common sense back into the beauty care industry," vows Shafi. This enthusiastic couple did not start Better Botanicals just to sell run-of-the-mill items. Instead, they aim to make a huge improvement in how people treat their skin. That is a tall order.

Shafi explains, "We want people to realize skin is a living, breathing organ that absorbs what you put on it. You shouldn't put anything on your skin that you wouldn't put in your mouth." Such a vision makes sense from a health point-of-view. Their vision also fires the first shot in a beauty products revolution. They are, in effect, tackling incredibly common beauty product myths to make a point, help people, and grow their business.

This married couple met while working in Europe where they led a rather glamorous corporate lifestyle. Shafi worked in marketing for Procter & Gamble and PepsiCo. Robert worked in Europe for the large Edelman public relations firm.

They were quoted in many business publications. Shafi even appeared in Pepsi promotional films in Europe.

Despite the glamor and fantastic corporate perks, they longed to do something quite different. Shafi commented on her Pepsi job by quipping, "How excited can you get selling brown, fizzy liquid?" For Robert, he longed to leave public relations, saying, "I wanted to get out of the service side of business. I wanted a product to sell that I believe in."

Shafi explained they realized, "Don't get stuck in a rut. If you find yourself stuck in a rut, climb out of it." The "rut" Shafi mentions is the comfort zone that pessimists never want to leave.

Robert commented that despite the risks they undertook in leaving fine corporate jobs, he and Shafi felt, "We'll always land on our feet." Such confidence is customary in optimistic people. It helps them jump into new endeavors knowing deep in their hearts that they will figure out how to come out on top.

Like optimists, Robert and Shafi brought their fabulous expertise with them. But now, instead of marketing soft drinks or publicizing other companies' products, the duo puts their expertise into Better Botanicals. Shafi's marketing know-how plus her knowledge of beauty products made using Ayurvedic medicine methods led to their products. These unique products help create a new and growing consumer desire for natural beauty products.

Robert's public relations expertise has helped them grow Better Botanicals without advertising. Instead, they grow their venture via publicity and word-of-mouth. Apparently, they are doing quite well, given the business' growth and its enthusiastic mentions in magazines like *Elle*, *Mirabella*, *Self*, and *Vogue*.

On the outside they look like a supremely confident couple. But, like most optimists, they are like ducks floating in a lake: They appear quite poised on the outside, but you do not see that underwater they are paddling furiously to move in the direction they want to go.

They described to us many troubles they have handled. For instance, they encountered glitches coordinating a number of key start-up events that could have derailed pessimistic souls. But, they pulled everything together in the nick of time using ingenuity and hard work. Robert observed that handling myriad obstacles in innovative ways taught them "not to limit yourself to just one option." That certainly sounds like wise advice in personal and work life, doesn't it?

We always find it fascinating to discover the attitudes of optimistic people who make a difference in the world. When we asked, the couple credited the following attitudes as proving tremendously helpful:

- ◆ "Hard work, honesty and passion will always deliver results. It's our basic work ethic." (Shafi)
- ◆ "Personal responsibility for success or failure" (Robert)
- ◆ "When we do something, we don't do it halfway" (Shafi)
- ◆ "View obstacles not as setbacks. They're like potholes. You either pave over them or go around them. But, obstacles are not setbacks. They're the norm to be handled." (Robert)

Their attitudes display many of the optimistic attitudes you learned throughout this book. This dynamic couple's assumptions on the work ethic, taking total self-responsibility, persistence, and focusing on solutions — not problems — ooze the sort of optimistic attitudes that can help you go far.

What words, phrases or affirmations fuel their optimism? Shafi and Robert told us the following are incredibly useful each day:

- ◆ "Think big" (Shafi)

- ◆ "Don't be afraid to make a mistake — *once*"
  (Shafi and Robert)
- ◆ "Turn negatives into positives; every problem
  has in it the grains of a more perfect solution"
  (Shafi)
- ◆ "Build a cathedral" (Robert)

Robert said they adore saying, "Build a cathedral." When
we asked what that means, he told us a story he found quite
compelling:

> *A man is walking down a country road, and comes
> across a field in which three men are breaking up
> large boulders with sledgehammers. He asks the first
> one what he is doing. The first man answers: "Can't
> you see? I'm breaking stones!" He asks the second
> man, who says: "Can't you see? I'm doing my job!"
> To the same question, the third man responds: "Can't
> you see? I'm building a cathedral!"*

Imagine going through *your* life "Building a cathedral."
Frequently uttering a snappy, fun to say, meaningful affirmation like "Build a cathedral" conveys a powerful message
to yourself and everyone around you. Plus, this exquisite
phrase gives a clear message about expecting the best *and*
working toward it.

We also felt impressed with their affirmation of "Think
big." Optimistic people create exciting visions of doing something *big* and wonderful. This could be in developing a business, achieving career success, or building a great family.
Dedicated optimists feel zest when they "Think big." In sharp
contrast, pessimists are pleased (they never are happy!) to
just get by.

A person's choice of role models also reveals a lot about
what inspires them. When we asked, Shafi immediately cited
her parents. From them, she learned, "Keep my eyes on the

big picture and know hard work, honesty and passion will reap rewards." She also credits the composer Beethoven as a role model. Shafi explained, "He was deaf when he wrote the wonderful symphony *Ode to Joy*. Where there's a will, there's a way. Just focus on your goals."

Robert told us a key role model was Lou Hughes of General Motors. He met Lou in Europe when Robert worked at the American Chamber of Commerce. At that time, Lou was head of GM's Opel division in Europe and on the board of the American Chamber of Commerce in Germany. Robert said that despite Lou's lofty position, "He showed respect for everyone. During a plant tour, he walked up to many employees. He knew each one's name, and he spoke personally with many of them. He treated all his employees equally, regardless of their level in the company."

This conveys a valuable lesson. A key part of achieving your vision and goals is securing the enthusiastic cooperation of many people. Optimists tend to be more outgoing than pessimists. Perhaps part of that is because optimists are more likely to help others feel special. In turn, those people are more likely to help the optimists who make them feel good. This creates a delightful cycle that assists optimists both personally and professionally.

In fact, Michael discovered this in his "benchmarking" research of successful and unsuccessful employees in many companies. Specifically, high-achievers tend to score higher on the Teamwork scale of the *Behavior Forecaster*™ test than their underachieving co-workers.* Robert's admiration for Lou Hughes illustrates the importance of actively nurturing teamwork and harmony in daily actions.

---

* You can take the *Behavior Forecaster*™ test and get your scores and a computerized report on how you stack up on 3 interpersonal skills, 5 personality traits, and 5 work motivations. To do this, see the "Materials You Can Order" section near the back of this book.

This vibrant, energetic couple sounded confident and cheerful when we interviewed them. They have accomplished a lot. Now, they set their sights on two key objectives. In business, they plan to boost both national and international distribution of their unique herbal skin, hair, bath, body, and aromatherapy products.

In their relationship, they are building a family; Shafi was seven months pregnant when we interviewed this loving couple. She summed it up by saying, "We work on having both a fruitful life and a successful business."

Making the World Literate:

Judith Bliss

Supremely optimistic and successful people create exciting visions *and* turn them into reality. A magnificent example of this is Judith Bliss, founder of Mindplay in Tucson, Arizona. Judith's vision is to make "a literate society." That is a huge vision — and Judith may be the person to make it possible.

Her latest computerized educational software is *Larrabee's Bridge to Adult Literacy*. Judith explains, "This new literacy product takes people reading at the first grade level and gets them up the the twelfth grade level in just 40-60 hours."

She explained, "Real growth is when you heal your own weakness of a flaw or skill you don't have. And when you fix that, it's awesome. My reading skills were agonizingly slow. By developing this product, I helped myself."

"I had difficulty reading as a child. Also, my son had dyslexia and he, too, had difficulty reading. I figured there must be an easy way to read. I discovered a reading system that works. So, I computerized this system."

For example, Judith tried the *Larabee's Bridge to Adult Literacy* on a 16 year old drop-out. He came to Judith two or three times a week for two hours per session. In five weeks, he got up to the eleventh grade reading level.

Importantly, Judith views learning as a pathway to improved self-esteem. For instance, the 16 year old "also improved his appearance and social skills. He got a job, and went back to school. By improving very fast, a person changes how they view themselves. This increases their confidence level."

Not only does Judith's vision enable her to help many people learn and boost their self-confidence, she also displays other optimism traits that prove crucial in life and in business. When we asked her about difficulties she has encountered, she laughed and indicated she certainly knows what it is like, figuratively, to hit a brick wall.

Most people want their business to grow all the time. If placed on a graph, they want their business to grow at a 45-degree angle. That would represent steady sales and profit growth all the time. But, Judith says her Mindplay company "grows like a picket fence — up and down. When my business hits a valley, I look at the valley as the best part. Why? Because when I hit the worst part, then I know I'm going to go up. That's when I get really creative."

She sums up a basic life choice as follows: "You can look at a valley or slump as the end of the world or as the beginning."

As we spoke with Judith, it struck us that creativity and ingenuity are hallmarks of her success. For example, as a young person with reading difficulties, she majored in math, so she would not need much reading skill.

Then, she worked for a company that sold expensive software for large mainframe-type computers. When she predicted personal computers would become more useful than huge mainframe computers, she left her job. On an airplane trip, she met an educational publisher. She agreed to design a computerized learning program for the publisher to sell. She worked doggedly on it. This paid off. She helped the publisher sell a lot of her basic reading and math programs, and "bought my first Jaguar!" Her *Math Magic* and *Easy Street* (for math and reading skills) educational software have helped huge numbers of people over many years.

Such an optimistic, "Can-Do" philosophy also helps Judith in her personal life. She explained to us difficulties she overcame personally, and commented, "Every time I have a failure, I have the opportunity to say, `What did I learn that can make me happier?'"

As you read throughout this book, a key to optimism is to hold upbeat attitudes. Judith told us her five key attitudes are the following:

◆ Persistence
◆ Curiosity
◆ Acceptance
◆ Hard work
◆ Playfulness

We asked Judith what she means by "acceptance?" She explained, "I never waste time on `I coulda, I woulda, I shoulda.' Instead, I just accept whatever happens and move on from there."

Suggestion: The next time you whimper, "I coulda, I woulda, I shoulda," cut it out. Quit wallowing in what you might have done. Instead, do something useful: Focus on solving your predicament or improving your situation.

Judith also gave us a fascinating insight into what she means by "persistence." She told us that on the road to her big accomplishment — her groundbreaking literacy software — she felt *driven*. I had a *mission*. It all came together in this product. Now, I feel very peaceful."

You read how your exciting vision — what Judith calls "mission" — fuels your motivation. In Judith's case she says the same thing, namely, she felt "driven" to reach her vision. That kept her going for years. Would she have reached her vision if she gave up along the way, or let herself run out of steam?

It proves eye-opening to find out key phrases or affirmations that optimistic, successful people say to themselves, so we asked Judith. Her key phrases or affirmations are

- ◆ "I think I can, I think I can."
- ◆ "If this is hard, I'm on the wrong track. I need to find other ways of getting there."
- ◆ "I've already done the hard part, so the next step will be easy."

The first phrase Judith mentioned to us derives from the fairy tale of *The Little Train that Could*. In this story, a little train needs to climb up a mountain. Despite the difficulties and some doubters, the train repeatedly recited its affirmation, "I think I can, I think I can." And the train did succeed!

We consider Judith's choice of the line from *The Little Train that Could* to be quite interesting. Michael has done a lot of testing and in-depth interviewing of candidates for executive positions. One of the many question he has asked many times is, "What story did you adore the most when you were a kid? And tell me the story."

Michael has found the most frequent childhood story cited by *highly successful* executives is *The Little Train that Could*. This pops up so very often that it seems like optimistic, accomplished people find this story symbolically expresses one of their deepest beliefs about how to live: A person with a strong "Can-Do" approach to life plus lots of hard work winds up on top — regardless of "mountains" the person must climb.

What is her next exciting vision? Judith confidently mentioned that she now aims to "help lots of people grow. I'm already watching a lot of people grow using my literacy product." Along the way, she probably will achieve another part of her dream — boosting people's self-confidence as they, perhaps for the first time, learn that they can learn.

Saving the Healthcare System:

Randy Preston

How's this for a big, exciting vision: Randy Preston started his Delphi Card® company in Cary, Illinois, "to give control of healthcare back to the American people, rather than let it be controlled by big healthcare and insurance companies."

A huge healthcare problem is that consumers — people going to physicians and other healthcare providers — do not personally pay for healthcare. Instead, employers pay for it through buying insurance or involvments in healthcare organizations. Then, employees go for treatment and, in effect, spend someone else's money for healthcare. It almost is like giving consumers a blank check and saying they can spend money without having to pay out of their own pockets. This explains much of the reason healthcare costs escalated and seem out of control.

Randy brilliantly aims to change this trend by helping consumers using his Delphi Card® healthcare payment system hold down expenses. This is done by providing employees with a tremendous amount of healthcare customer service and education. This proves vastly different than typical services provided by insurance or healthcare organizations.

For example, one company that just started using Randy's system had an employee who went to a chiroprac-

---

Delphi Card® is a registered trademark of The Preston Group, Inc. in Cary, Illinois.

tor 29 times in one year. So, one of Randy's staff nurses visited the company to observe the employee working. The nurse noticed the employee

◆ weighed 300 pounds
◆ lifted very heavy objects
◆ had shoe soles worn out at an angle, so his feet were not flat on the floor
◆ worked on a very worn-out mat

These observations explained why the employee had foot, leg, and back complaints — and spent big amounts of money on a chiropractor. So, Randy's company arranged for the employee to get

◆ new work shoes
◆ new mat
◆ fruit, instead of candy and sweetrolls, as company-provided snacks

The results have been outstanding. The employee

◆ is healthier and does not need a chiropractor
◆ is more productive on-the-job
◆ spends less healthcare dollars

Most insurance or healthcare companies would have focused solely on paying for treatment and reducing costs by terminating treatment. In sharp contrast, Randy's Delphi Card® company dove in, uncovered the problem's cause, and helped the employee overcome the trouble. This is a rather revolutionary approach to healthcare.

Randy pointed out, "The highest quality healthcare costs the least. This includes proper diet, exercise, sleep, and an all around healthy lifestyle."

We have known Randy for years. While he is doing quite well now, we also know he went through rough patches. For instance, shortly before starting Delphi Card®, Randy worked at a fast-growing health insurance company that hit the skids and went belly up.

Randy handled this shocking experience like a true optimist. He told us,

> *After that company went bust, I hit bottom. I could have stayed home and felt depressed. But, instead, I got a job driving a limo, because I knew I'd meet executives driving in the limo, and I could talk to them to get advice and potential business. I actually cried while driving that limo. I had a newborn daughter, and my wife was upset. So, between customers I wrote my business plan on the front seat of the limo. I would discuss my plans with the corporate executives I drove. Some of them later became clients of Delphi Card®. I used my time well. I kept planning, learning and selling from the front seat of the limo.*

Randy's way of handing a downturn shows a key quality of optimists. As we taught you, optimistic individuals continually pick themselves up over and over again, regardless of how many times they fall down or get pushed down. Randy surely did that. We also know that after Randy started his business he hit a number of brick walls that would have discouraged a less persistent person. But, Randy keeps picking himself up, as we recommended earlier, "exactly one more time."

Randy always impresses us as a supremely optimistic, buoyant person. He told us his chief attitudes are
- "Persistence" and "stick-to-itiveness"
- "Belief in my ideas"
- "Discipline"
- "Knowing what I'm doing is right for both the healthcare business and for helping people be healthier and more responsible for their lives"

We probed what Randy meant by "discipline." He explained,

> *I follow my vision and plan no matter what happens. Even if I get rejected 20 times today, I wake up tomorrow and go at it again and could get rejected 20 more times. Then, I still wake up the next day, and keep doing it. I never perceive it as rejection per se. Instead, I say to myself that prospects who reject me understood one of my five points. The next time I contact them, they'll understand two points. Eventually, they'll understand the usefulness of the Delphi Card® method and buy into it.*

As with the other optimistic, successful people we interviewed, Randy also shows the importance of making a plan and keeping to it — regardless of obstacles encountered. Like Randy is fond of saying, "Always keep your vision in sight."

Randy often uses a few phrases to keep himself buoyed up. These are proverbs you may have heard, including

- "Measure twice, cut once."
- "An ounce of prevention is worth a pound of cure."
- "If it was easy, everyone would be doing it."
- "Even a blind hog stumbles onto an acorn from time to time."

When we asked Randy about why he considers the first two proverbs important, he told us, "I need to make sure I have reasons to feel confident before I take action. I don't do anything half-baked!" As you learned in this book, it is not enough to just feel confident. You need to do your homework and then take action. By doing so, you have sensible reasons to feel confident as you run after your vision and goals.

The "blind hog" stumbling "onto an acorn" intrigued us. Randy revealed, "I've gotten a lot of rejection for my product, but I keep persisting and, from time to time, I make a sale." This strikes us as very typical of optimistic people who keep persisting. Optimists know deep in their hearts that they will come out on top if they just keep plugging away. It is this belief that enables someone to keep going long after a pessimistic person would have given up or wallowed in self-pity.

Randy mentioned a few role models from whom he learned valuable lessons. His first role model, whom he never met, is Norman Vincent Peale, author of *The Power of Positive Thinking* and other inspirational books. From Dr. Peale, Randy learned, "I have a *choice:* I can see the positive in things or the negative. I choose to focus on the positive."

Another role model was a World Book Encyclopedia salesman Randy met while in grammar school. Randy would tag along after this salesman, watching how he sold. From him, Randy gleaned, "People buy from people, not from companies."

Finally, Randy mentioned his sports coach in high school would "scream, yell, and rant." As Randy described this wild, demeaning person, we could not imagine what he learned, so we asked. He revealed, "I learned people express themselves in different ways." Notice what Randy did that is so wonderfully typical of optimists. A pessimistic person would have felt blown away by a screaming, yelling authority figure. Instead, Randy distilled a fabulously helpful lesson out of this. He, as the adage goes, turned a lemon into lemonade.

Now that Randy has attained many of his goals, what is his vision for his future? Randy's vision is to have over one million healthcare consumers carrying a Delphi Card® smart card. A smart card in the hands of healthcare consumers will act as a

- ◆ debit, credit and charge card to pay for healthcare at the time of service

◆ way to collect data on a person's healthcare history

Such data will help Delphi Card®'s staff nurses intervene to make sure the consumer receives the most effective help for his or her healthcare concerns. For instance, earlier we described the example of a person who went to a chiropractor 29 times in the year before Randy's company started providing his healthcare management. By using this data, Randy's staff nurses helped the person solve medical problems, become more productive, and reduce healthcare expenses.

His vision links technology and personalized consumer service to innovative healthcare management. Randy certainly appears to be a person who can help millions of people live happier, healthier, and more productive lives.

Bringing the Finest Chocolates to the World:

Fran Bigelow

If you love fine chocolate, you could be a fan of Fran Bigelow's products. She founded Fran's Chocolates 15 years ago in Seattle. She has two stores and a booming mail order business. You also can buy Fran's exquisite chocolates at the finest stores, such as Williams-Sonoma and Neiman Marcus. In fact, if you go to a Starbucks coffee shop, you can enjoy Fran's chocolates there, too.

As with most optimistic people, Fran started with an exciting vision, namely, "To set up the *finest* chocolate store in the U.S." Notice that Fran did not want to start a regular chocolate store. Like successful, optimistic people, she aimed to create something absolutely outstanding, the *"finest."*

As you read earlier in this book, optimistic and successful people aim for the stars, while their less accomplished counterparts are pleased just to keep their feet on the ground. Fran aimed for the stars and, in the world of fine chocolate, certainly has hit the stars. Here is proof: Fran proudly told us that one of her thrilling accomplishments was being recognized as the best chocolatier in America in *The Book of Chocolate.*

When we asked Fran to discuss her vision, she emphasized she wanted to "create an environment to bring small pleasures into people's lives. I believe the marvelous taste of fine chocolate inspires a passion and brings a magic to people. I want to give people something out of the ordinary. My vision includes moving people to a higher level or standard of taste."

While Fran obviously is doing quite well now, she did need to successfully tackle obstacles along the way. When we asked her to tell us about a horrible experience she encountered, she immediately told us how in her sixth year of business she landed a big order for very special chocolates. After much work perfecting the recipe and production, her company made all the chocolates ordered.

Just then, something earth-shattering happened: The company that placed this huge, specialized order cancelled the order! For a pessimistic soul, this could have been emotionally devastating plus financially dreadful.

But Fran decided to turn this problem into an opportunity — a tactic employed by optimistic people. Instead of licking her wounds and suffering the loss, Fran sent these magnificent, very special chocolates to prospective customers. Lo and behold, a manager at Williams-Sonoma felt incredibly impressed with the samples Fran sent to him. He called Fran, oohed and ahhed over Fran's fine chocolates, and placed Williams-Sonoma's first order for chocolates. That started a long-term business relationship between Fran's Chocolates and the highly respected Williams-Sonoma chain of food and cookware stores. Fran turned possible defeat into real victory. She sums up part of her philosophy with her comment, "I don't get immobilized by fear that an obstacle is large."

Optimistic people exude confident attitudes. Fran mentioned her most important attitudes are the following:

◆ "Determination"
◆ "Can-Do attitude"
◆ "To keep a spark in my life, I keep learning new things."
◆ "Value creativity and learning"
◆ Resourcefulness: "I'm always able to find an answer. And if I don't, I can find someone who can find the answer."

A couple phrases Fran often uses also illustrate how she uses certain optimistic affirmations to help her and her staff keep plugging away. Two of her favorites are

◆ "We can do it"
◆ "We can meet any challenge — and we do!"

As you learned in this book, role models teach people important lessons about how to live a confident, forward moving life. Fran credits Josephine Araldo, one of her first cooking instructors, with being one of Fran's chief role models. From Josephine, Fran learned this lesson: "You can take any dish and make it successful. You can turn any ingredients into magic. If things start to go wrong, you can always fix it." Those sound like super-helpful words for cooking in particular and, importantly, wise words for living in general.

Fran also credited two "inspirational speakers" as helping her make profound improvements in how she tackles situations. For instance, motivational speaker Lou Tice taught Fran about visualizing what she wants to achieve before she goes for it. From Lou, Fran learned, "When I can see my dream, I can march toward it. Once I did see my dream in my mind, I was able to open my first store!"

Also, motivational speaker W. Mitchell conveyed a magnificently useful lesson to Fran. Mitchell was in horrible accidents which left him physically challenged in a number of ways. Yet, as we know, his spirit and "Can-Do" attitude could light up the night. From W. Mitchell, Fran told us she learned, "It's not what happens to you, it's what you do about it."

We spent an entire chapter helping you to become a great role model. Fran's optimistic approach to life has positively impacted her children. In fact, they keep telling her she is a wonderful role model. Fran summarizes her children's admiration for her by saying they learned from Fran's example "to set your sights on your goals, keep working toward them, and you can do it." She adds, "They also see it takes lots of hard work."

Earlier in the book, we cited a fascinating *Worth* magazine article reporting on research of people in the top one percent, in terms of net worth.[1] The top 1-percenters overwhelmingly are self-made millionaires. The survey revealed top 1-percenters primarily credit these two factors as "very important" in success:

- ◆ tremendous persistence (82%)
- ◆ encouraging spouse (72%)

Fran's husband is a very supportive spouse. She describes him as "an optimistic, upbeat person. He encourages me." Of course, people succeed without an encouraging spouse. But, having one provides a tremendous cheerleader on the road to health, prosperity, and happiness.

For the next few years, Fran's exciting vision is to "Bring our chocolates to a wider audience." Her three goals to accomplish this include opening a certain number of new retail stores, teaching the rare art of hand-making fine chocolates to more employees, and expanding her already success-ful mail order business.

Revolutionizing Water:

David Marcheschi

David Marcheschi solved a huge quandary for millions of people, namely, "How can I consume caffeine — an immensely popular perk-you-up chemical — without consuming cola or coffee?" David's brilliant solution: Combine the health benefits of bottled water with caffeine. This resulted in his Water Joe® coffee and cola alternative.

David explains Water Joe® is "The first caffeine-enhanced natural water ever produced. One bottle of our 16.9 ounce natural water is equivalent to one cup of coffee. If people don't like the taste of coffee or colas, or if they're sick of the sugars, calories or carbonation in colas, this would be an alternative beverage for them." In its first few years, David's product already is distributed in all 50 states and a few foreign nations.

In talking with David, we felt extremely impressed with his strong belief that his product would help many people. But with minimal advertising dollars, David also realized he needed to get the word out. So, he focuses his marketing efforts on obtaining publicity in the media. He does this exceedingly well. As we mentioned earlier, in *Alice in Wonderland*, Alice asks the Cheshire Cat, "Where do I begin?" The Cheshire Cat replies, "Well, my dear, you begin at the beginning."

Water Joe® is a registered trademark of David Marcheschi, Water Concepts, L.L.C., Chicago, Illinois.

That is exactly what David did. He persistently contacted the editor at his hometown suburban newspaper. Finally, the editor wrote a wonderful article on David in the newspaper. From there, David kept pursuing publicity for Water Joe®. Eventually, an article written about David and his "coffee/cola alternative" caught the attention of a *New York Times* reporter. The resulting *New York Times* article set off a chain reaction of publicity that would make the most seasoned public relations expert drool. So far, David has had articles about himself and Water Joe® in major publications, including *New York Times, Newsweek, Time, Success,* and *Chicago Tribune. USA Today* newspaper awarded Water Joe® its prestigious "Product of the Year" award. Reuters and Associated Press newswires have carried articles to publications across the world. That's not all. David also has been interviewed on major television shows at ABC, CBS, CNBC, CNN, and NBC.

All this started with David's exciting vision for his Water Joe® product to "Provide people with a coffee/cola alternative." Think about that. As you learned in this book, your vision must be big and exciting. Imagine the excitement exuded by, in effect, creating a revolutionary beverage.

He must be doing something right. "Now, we get a lot of mail from people saying they enjoy our unique concept. I had a belief I could change people's lifestyles. Once I could get Water Joe® on the shelves and hear the praise, I knew all my trials and tribulations would be worthwhile."

When we asked David about his most important attitudes leading to his achievements, he focused on two:

◆ "Very persistent"
◆ "Strong belief" in his product's usefulness

As you read earlier, persistence is a hallmark of optimistic people. It is not enough just to have an exciting vision and goals. You also must keep plugging away to turn your vision into reality.

David certainly shows tremendous persistence in the face of formidable obstacles. For instance, he started with a great idea for a new product — but no money to fund it. After working out details of the product, David decided to find a water bottler to make the product and also, hopefully, provide money to launch Water Joe®. While working two years full-time as a mortgage broker, David created time to make presentations to many, many bottlers. However, for two years, the bottlers kept throwing "No!!" in his face. Finally, he found a bottler willing to produce Water Joe® plus provide funds to help get the venture off the ground.

This and other experiences David told us illustrates how his persistence paid off. It took David two years of "strong belief" in his product and making pitches to bottlers before he got his venture off the ground. What would have happened if David stopped after one year and 11 months?

Also, as mentioned earlier, David kept running after the editor of his local suburban newspaper to write a story about him and his new product. The editor refused many times. Finally, the editor agreed to write the article. It was a great article that was reprinted in other suburban newspapers. That helped launch David's media blitz to publicize Water Joe®.

What would have happened if David did not persist by repeatedly calling that editor? Many people would not persist the way David has. And that explains why many people with fantastic ideas have only an idea — but nothing tangible — to show for it.

We also asked David about words or key phrases he finds helpful. David enthusiastically responded that he reads and thinks about a number of "phrases and quotes every chance I get each day." For example, David especially likes this phrase: "When I go through a low, there will be a lesson." This is someone who certainly does learn from experience. He also cherishes this quote from T.E. Lawrence:

Those who dream by the night in the dusty recesses
of their minds wake in the day to find that all was
vanity; but the dreamers of the day are dangerous
men, for they may act their dreams with open eyes
and make it possible.

Also, role models have played a key role in David's life.
Interestingly, David does not personally know any of the role
models he finds so special. Instead, he finds his role models
in books and articles he reads about successful people. For
example, he admires Ben and Jerry of ice cream fame, based
on reading a book they wrote. From them, David learned,
"There always has to be a moral ethic to my business."

Toward this end, David donates his Water Joe® to an extremely sick poor person whose physician recommended
Water Joe® to help her keep up her blood pressure. Also, it
has been found that caffeine helps hyperactive children. So,
David has become active in an association that focuses on
such concerns. Doing so can help expand the market for Water
Joe®, while also helping parents and children in a unique way.

Importantly, David has served as a role model. "By seeing my success with Water Joe®, I've had friends who have
gone on to try various businesses that they thought about
but never did before. By seeing me, it gives them inspiration
to go for their dreams and start their own businesses."

Near the beginning of this book, you learned one of the
five quickest ways to become optimistic is to be a role model.
Near the end of this book, we even devoted an entire chapter
to how you can be a tremendous role model for your family,
friends, and co-workers. David's activities have done this
quite well for people who previously hesitated to attempt to
turn their visions into reality.

Another way in which David displays characteristics of
a classic optimist is that he *writes* exactly what he wants. For

example, he told us this example of how useful such writing is:

> *A number of years ago, I made a list of what I wanted to accomplish, like buying a computer and a new car. I also listed financial and social goals. I read my list every day for about 60 days. Then, I put the list away. The next year, I picked up my list and looked at it. I was amazed that I accomplished almost everything on my list. I conditioned or programmed my mind to achieve what I wanted.*

David's example illustrates a suggestion we gave to you. Put into writing what you want to accomplish. Keep reading this as you plug away. By reading your goals, you can, like David, "condition or program" your mind to achieve what you most want.

As David looks into the future, his chief objectives are to grow his Water Joe® business, land even more international distribution, plus spend more time on his social life. This final objective for his social life is useful for you to see. We suggested you include a "balance" goal for yourself. This helps you achieve your exciting vision, as you also build a delightful personal life. However, at times you may need to focus primarily on your key goals — persist like David so strikingly does — before you can devote much of your valuable time and energy to achieving your goal for a balanced lifestyle.

16

So, What Did You Learn?

You read this book to learn how to boost your optimism. In brief, an optimistic person

- possesses a clear vision of an exciting, meaning-ful life
- works on goals to help progress toward his or her exciting vision
- has a confident, "Can-Do" attitude
- exerts personal control over his or her life
- takes high levels of self-responsibility
- is outgoing
- lives a prosperous life

Importantly, motivational books you may have read preached that you should display positive attitudes. However, they seldom *proved* to you that their techniques really work.

Fortunately, we provide to you over 30 years combined experience as psychologists plus numerous research studies that show you throughout this book that optimism

- positively affects your health, prosperity, and happiness
- is easy to learn

Jointly, we developed a unique Intensive Coaching^{SM} method that helps clients quicker (in only 3 - 6 hours, usually) and more profoundly than typical counseling procedures. Also, we deliver over 100 speeches and workshops annually. Our presentations help groups of people exceed their own expectations. As such, our book reveals to you special techniques we use.

The methods we showed you have equipped large numbers of people to boost their optimism and success in both their personal and work lives. Now, you also can benefit from our extensive professional expertise that has helped so many people achieve health, prosperity, and happiness.

We invite you to contact us to let us know how this book has helped you *achieve your wildest dreams*.

Positively,

Michael W. Mercer, Ph.D. & Maryann V. Troiani, Psy.D.

Bibliography

Chapter 1

1. David Myers & Edward Diener, "The New Scientific Pursuit of Happiness," *The Harvard Mental Health Letter*, August 1997, Vol. 14, No. 2, pages 4-7.
2. T. Kohler & C. Haimerl, "Daily Stress as a Trigger of Migraine Attacks: Results of Thirteen Single-Subject Studies," *Journal of Consulting & Clinical Psychology*, 1990, Vol. 58, pages 870-872.
3. P.R. Martin & H.M. Seneviratne, "Effects of Food Deprivation and a Stressor on Head Pain," *Health Psychology*, July 1997, Vol. 16, No. 4, pages 310-318.
4. J.A. Harrigan, J.R. Kues, D.F. Ricks & R. Smith, "Moods that Predict Coming Migraine Headaches," *Pain*, 1984, Vol. 20, pages 385-396.
5. O. Carlton Simonton, Stephanie Matthews-Simonton & James Creighton. *Getting Well Again: A Step-by-Step, Self-Help Guide to Overcoming Cancer for Patients and Their Families.* Los Angeles: J.P. Tarcher, Inc., 1978.
6. S.N. Haynes, L.R. Gannon, J. Bank, D. Shelton & J. Goodwin, "Caphalic Blood Flow Correlates of Induced Headaches," *Journal of Behavioral Medicine*, 1990, Vol. 13, pages 467-480.

7. Deepak Chopra, *Quantum Healing: Exploring the Frontiers of Mind/Body Medicine*. New York: Bantam Books, 1989.

8. Deepak Chopra, *Perfect Health. The Complete Mind/Body Guide*. New York: Harmony Books, 1991.

9. "Hearts and Minds - Part 2," *The Harvard Mental Health Letter*, August 1997, Vol. 14, No. 2, page 3.

10. C. Peterson, M. Seligman & G. Vaillant, "Pessimistic Explanatory Style as a Risk Factor for Physical Illnesses: A Thirty-Five Year Longitudinal Study," *Journal of Personality & Social Psychology*, 1988, Vol. 55, pages 23-27.

11. E.A. Bachen, S.B. Manuch, S. Cohen, M.F. Muldeon, R. Raible, T.B. Herbert & B.S. Rabin, "Adrenergic Blockade Ameliorates Cellular Immune Responses to Mental Stress in Humans," *Psychosomatic Medicine*, 1995, Vol. 57, pages 366-372.

12. J.K. Kiecolt-Glaser, J.T. Cacioppo, N.B. Malarkey & R. Glaser, "Acute Psychological Stressors and Short-Term Immune Changes: What, Why, for Whom and to What Extent?" *Psychosomatic Medicine*, 1992, Vol. 54, pages 680-685.

13. Bruno Cortis, *Heart & Soul: A Psychological & Spiritual Guide To Preventing & Healing Heart Disease*. New York: Villard Books, 1995.

14. *USA Today*, April 16, 1997, Section D, page 1.

15. Sheldon Cohen & colleagues, "Psychological Stress and Susceptibility to the Common Cold," *New England Journal of Medicine*, 1991, page 325.

16. J.S. Martindale & Maryann Troiani, "The Quantum Relationship between Brain Wave Frequency & Spectral Color Wavelengths of the Human Mind/Body Energy Field." Manuscript, Northeastern Illinois University, 1981.

17. J.S. Martindale, "Psychogenensis: A Theoretical Model in Psychophysics on the Origin of the Mind," 1978. Paper presented at the Parascience Institute, University College, London, England.
18. Marty Munson, Teresa A. Yeykal & Therese Walsh, "Mind Over Life Span," *Prevention*, June 1994, Vol. 46, No. 6, page 21.
19. Thomas J. Stanley & William D. Danko, *The Millionaire Next Door*. Atlanta, Georgia: Longstreet Press, 1996.
20. Richard Todd, "Who Me, Rich?" *Worth*, September 1977, pages 70-84.
21. Michael W. Mercer, *Behavior Forecaster*™ Test. Barrington, Illinois: Mercer Systems Inc., 1991 & 1997.
22. Michael W. Mercer, *Hire The Best — & Avoid The Rest*™. New York: Amacom, 1993.

Chapter 2

1. David Myers & Edward Diener, "The New Scientific Pursuit of Happiness," *The Harvard Mental Health Letter*, August 1997, Vol. 14, No. 2, pages 4-7.

Chapter 3

1. Lee Berk & Stanley Tan, "Humor as Medicine," *Hope Healthletter*, April 1997, page 1. Published by The Hope Heart Institute, Seattle, Washington.
2. Norman Cousins, *Anatomy of an Illness*. New York: Bantam, 1979.
2. Sid Kirchheimer, Gale Maleskey & colleagues, *Energy Force*. Emmaus, Pennsylvania: Rodale Press, 1997, pages 68-70.

3. Deepak Chopra, *Ageless Body, Timeless Mind: The Quantum Alternative to Growing Old.* New York: Harmony Books, 1993.

Chapter 4

1. Michael W. Mercer, *How Winners Do It: High Impact People Skills for Your Career Success.* Englewood Cliffs, New Jersey: Prentice Hall, 1994.

Chapter 6

1. J.F. Chaves & T.X. Barber, "Cognitive Strategies, Experimenter Modeling, and Expectation in the Attenuation of Pain," *Journal of Abnormal Psychology*, 1974, Vol. 83, pages 356-363.
2. M. Rosenbaum, "Individual Differences in Self-Control Behaviors and Tolerance of Painful Stimulation," *Journal of Abnormal Psychology*, 1980, Vol. 89, pages 581-590.
3. Yuichi Shoda, Walter Michel & Philip K. Peake, "Predicting Adolescent Cognitive & Self-Regulatory Competencies from Preschool Delay of Gratification," *Developmental Psychology*, 1990, Vol. 26, No. 6, pages 978-86.

Chapter 7

1. M.S. Rider, J.W. Floyd & J. Kirkpatrick, "The Effect of Music, Imagery and Relaxation on Adrenal Corticosteroids and the Re-entrainment of Circadian Rhythms," *Journal of Music Therapy*, 1985, Vol. 22, pages 46-58.
2. B. Wrangsjo & D. Korlin, "Guided Imagery and Music as a Psychotherapeutic Method in Psychiatry," *Journal of Association for Music and Imagery*, 1995, Vol. 4, pages 79-92.

Chapter 8

1. Michael W. Mercer, *How Winners Do It: High Impact People Skills for Your Career Success*. Englewood Cliffs, New Jersey: Prentice Hall, 1994.

Chapter 9

1. Deepak Chopra, *Perfect Health: The Complete Mind/Body Guide*. New York: Harmony Books, 1991, pages 109-110.
2. E.A. Bachen, S.B. Manuck, S. Cohen, T.B. Herbert & B.S. Rabin, "Adrenergic Blockade Ameliorates Cellular Immune Responses to Mental Stress in Humans," *Psychosomatic Medicine*, 1995, Vol. 57, pages 366-372.
3. J.K. Kiecolt-Glaser, J.T. Cacioppo, W.B. Malarkey & R. Glaser, "Acute Psychological Stressors and Short-Term Immune Changes: What, Why, for Whom and to What Extent?" *Psychosomatic Medicine*, 1992, Vol. 54, pages 680-685.
4. Howard Friedman & S. Boothby-Kewley, "The Disease-Prone Personality: A Meta-Analytic View," *American Psychologist*, 1987, Vol. 42.
5. Bruce McEwen & Eliot Stellar, "Stress and the Individual: Mechanisms Leading to Disease," *Archives of Internal Medicine*, September 1993, Vol. 153.
6. S.N. Haynes, L.R. Gannon, J. Bank, D. Shelton & J. Goodwin, "Cephalic Blood Flow Correlates of Induced Headaches," *Journal of Behavioral Medicine*, 1990, Vol.13, pages 467-480.
7. T. Kohler & C. Haimerl, "Daily Stress as a Trigger of Migraine Attacks: Results of 13 Single-Subject Studies," *Journal of Consulting and Clinical Psychology*, 1990, Vol. 58, pages 870-872.
8. P.R. Martin & H.M. Seneviratne, "Effects of Food Deprivation and a Stressor on Head Pain," *Health Psychology*, July 1997, Vol. 16, No. 4, pages 310-318.

9. J.A. Harrigan, J.R. Kues, D.F. Ricks & R. Smith, "Moods that Predict Coming Migraine Headaches," *Pain*, 1984, Vol. 20, pages 385-396.

10. Sheldon Cohen & colleagues, "Psychological Stress and Susceptibility to the Common Cold," *New England Journal of Medicine*, 1991, Vol. 325.

11. Robert Anda & colleagues, "Depressed Affect, Hopelessness, and the Risk of Ischemic Heart Disease in a Cohort of U.S. Adults," *Epidemiology*, July 1993.

12. Bruno Cortis, *Heart & Soul: A Psychological & Spriritual Guide to Preventing & Healing Heart Disease*. New York: Villard Book, 1995.

13. E.A. Bachen, S.B. Manuck, S. Cohen, T.B. Herbert & B.S. Rabin, "Adrenergic Blockade Ameliorates Cellular Immune Responses to Mental Stress in Humans," *Psychosomatic Medicine*, 1995, Vol. 57, pages 366-372.

14. J.K. Kiecolt-Glaser, J.T. Cacioppo, W.B. Malarkey & R. Glaser, "Acute Psychological Stressors and Short-Term Immune Changes: What, Why, for Whom and to What Extent?" *Psychosomatic Medicine*, 1992, Vol. 54, pages 680-685.

15. J.C. Courtney & colleagues, "Stressful Life Events and the Risk of Colorectal Cancer," *Epidemiology*, September 1993, Vol. 4, Number 5.

16. O. Carlton Simonton, Stephanie Matthews-Simonton & James Creighton. *Getting Well Again: A Step-by-Step, Self-Help Guide to Overcoming Cancer for Patients and Their Families*. Los Angeles: J.P. Tarcher, Inc., 1978, page 51.

17. J.W. Pennebaker, S.D. Barger & J. Tiebout, "Disclosure of Traumas and Health among Holocaust Survivors," *Psychosomatic Medicine*, 1989, Vol. 51, pages 577-589.

18. J.W. Pennebaker & S.K. Beall, "Confronting a Traumatic Event: Toward an Understanding of Inhibition and Disease," *Journal of Abnormal Psychology*, 1986, Vol. 95, pages 274-281.

19. J.W. Pennebaker & R.C. O'Heeron, "Confiding in Others and Illness Rate among Spouses of Suicide and Accidental-Death Victims," *Journal of Abnormal Psychology*, 1984, Vol. 93, pages 473-476.
20. J.W. Pennebaker & J.R. Susan, "Disclosure of Traumas and Psychosomatic Processes," *Social Science and Medicine*, 1988, Vol. 26, pages 327-332.
21. J.E. Kelley, Mark A. Lumley & J.C.C. Leisen, "Health Effects of Emotional Disclosure in Rheumatoid Arthritis Patients," *Health Psychology*, July 1997, Vol. 16, No. 4, pages 331-340.

Chapter 10

1. Daniel Goleman, *Emotional Intelligence*. New York: Bantam, 1995, pages 174-175.
2. A.V. McGrady, R. Yonker, S.Y. Tan, T.H. Fine & M. Woerner, "The Effect of Biofeedback-Assisted Relaxation Training on Blood Pressure and Selected Biochemical Parameters in Patients with Essential Hypertension," *Biofeedback and Self-Regulation*, 1981, Vol. 6, pages 343-353.
3. B. Wrangsjo & D. Korlin, "Guided Imagery and Music as a Psychotherapeutic Method in Psychiatry," *Journal of the Association for Music and Imagery*, 1995, Vol. 4, pages 79-92.
4. E.M. Jacobi, "The Efficacy of the Bonny Method of Guided Imagery and Music as Experiential Therapy in the Primary Care of Persons with Rheumatoid Arthritis," 1994, Unpublished doctoral dissertation, Union Institute, Cincinnati, Ohio.
5. C.H. McKinney, M.H. Antoni, A. Kumar & M. Kumar, "The Effects of Guided Imagery and Music (GIM) on Depression and Beta-Endorphin in Healthy Adults: A Pilot Study," *Journal of the Association for Music and Imagery*, 1995, Vol.4, pages 67-78.

6. C.H. McKinney, M.H. Antoni, M. Kumar, F.C. Tims, and P.M. McCabe, "Effects of Guided Imagery and Music (GIM) Therapy on Mood and Cortisol in Healthy Adults," *Health Psychology*, July 1997, Vol. 16, No. 4, pages 390-400.

7. F.S. Goldberg, "The Bonny Method of Guided Imagery and Music." In T. Wigram, B. Saperston & R. West (Eds.), *The Art and Science of Music Therapy: A Handbook*. Chur, Switzerland: Harwood Academic, 1995. pages 112-124.

8. R.L. Blake & S.R. Bishop, "The Bonny Method of Guided Imagery and Music (GIM) in the Treatment of Post-Traumatic Stress Disorder (PTSD) with Adults in a Psychiatric Setting," *Music Therapy Perspectives*, 1995, Vol. 12, pages 125-129.

9. C.H. McKinney, M.H. Antoni, M. Kumar, F.C. Tims, and P.M. McCabe, "Effects of Guided Imagery and Music (GIM) Therapy on Mood and Cortisol in Healthy Adults," *Health Psychology*, July 1997, Vol. 16, No. 4, pages 390-400.

10. C.H. McKinney, M.H. Antoni, M. Kumar, F.C. Tims, and P.M. McCabe, "Effects of Guided Imagery and Music (GIM) Therapy on Mood and Cortisol in Healthy Adults," *Health Psychology*, July 1997, Vol. 16, No. 4, page 392.

11. M.F. Clark & L.H. Keiser, *Teaching Guided Imagery and Music: An Experiential/Didactic Approach*. Olney, Maryland: Archedigm, 1989.

12. J.S. Martindale & Maryann V. Troiani, "The Quantum Relationship between Brain Wave Frequency and Spectral Color Wavelengths of the Human Mind/Body Energy Field." Manuscript, Northeastern Illinois University, 1981.

Chapter 11

1. John Ott, *Health & Light*. Greenwich, Connecticut: The Devin-Adair Company, 1973.
2. Jacob Liberman, *Light: Medicine of the Future*. Santa Fe, New Mexico: Bear and Company Publishing, 1991, pages 10-11, page 20, and pages 122-123.
3. Zane Kime, *Sunlight*. Penryn, California: World Health Publications, 1980.
4. Fritz Hollwich, *The Influence of Ocular Light Perception and Metabolism in Man and Animal*. New York: Spring-Verlag, 1979.
5. John Ott, *Health and Light*. Greenwich, Connecticut: The Devin-Adair Company, 1973.
6. John Ott, *Light Radiation and You*. Greenwich, Connecticut: The Devin-Adair Company, 1982.
7. John Ott, "Color and Light: Their Effects on Plants, Animals, and People - Part 1," *Journal of Biosocial Research*, 1985, Vol. 7.
8. John Ott, "Color and Light: Their Effects on Plants, Animals, and People - Part 4," *Journal of Biosocial Research*, 1988, Vol. 10, pages 111-116, pages 126-127.
9. N.E. Rosenthal, *Seasons of Mind*. New York: Bantam Books, 1989.
10. N.E. Rosenthal, "Seasonal Affective Disorder: A Description of the Syndrome and Preliminary Findings with Light Therapy," *Archives of General Psychiatry*, 1984, Vol. 41, pages 72-80.
11. Jacob Liberman, *Light: Medicine of the Future*. Santa Fe, New Mexico: Bear and Company Publishing, 1991.
12. N.E. Rosenthal, *Seasons of Mind*. New York: Bantam Books, 1989.
13. Linaya Hahn, *PMS: Solving the Puzzle*. Evanston, Illinois: Chicago Spectrum Press, 1995, page 95.

14. William Crook, *The Yeast Connection: A Medical Breakthrough.* New York: Vintage Books, 1996, page 9 and pages 17-39.
15. William Crook, *The Yeast Connection: A Medical Breakthrough.* New York: Vintage Books, 1996, page 9 and pages 17-39.
16. William Crook, *The Yeast Connection: A Medical Breakthrough.* New York: Vintage Books, 1996, pages 17-39.

Chapter 12

1. Thomas J. Stanley & Williams D. Danko, *The Millionaire Next Door.* Atlanta, Georgia: Longstreet Press, 1996.
2. Thomas J. Stanley & Williams D. Danko, *The Millionaire Next Door.* Atlanta, Georgia: Longstreet Press, 1996, page 28.
3. David Brindley, "Ten Pros Pick 30 Funds: Where Top Managers Stash Their Retirement Cash," *U.S. News & World Report,* June 9, 1997, pages 95-103.
4. Tod Barnhart, *The Five Rituals of Wealth.* New York: Harper Collins, 1995, page 23.
5. *Target 5 Trust.* Lisle, IL: Nike Securities, 1997.
6. Harvey Knowles, III & Damon Petty, *The Dividend Investor: A Safe & Sure Way To Beat The Market with High-Yield Dividend Stocks.* Burr Ridge, IL: Irwin, 1992.

Chapter 13

1. Carole Hoover, Lynn Katz & John Gottman, "The Family as a Meta-Emotion Culture," *Cognition & Emotions,* Spring 1994.
2. Martin Seligman, *The Optimistic Child.* New York: Harper Collins, 1996.

3. *Heart Start: The Emotional Foundations of School Readiness Programs.* Arlington, Virginia: National Center for Clinical Infant Programs, 1992.
4. D. McClelland, J. Atkinson, R. Clark & E. Lowell, *The Achievement Motive.* New York: Appleton-Century-Crofts, 1953.

Materials You Can Order

Books

Print quantity you want on line provided.

_____ *How Winners Do It: High Impact People Skills for Your Career Success* by Michael W. Mercer
Price: $25
❑ Check here if you want Michael to autograph to you

_____ *Hire the Best — & Avoid the Rest*™ by Michael Mercer
Price: $25
❑ Check here if you want Michael to autograph to you

_____ *Change Your Underwear — Change Your Life*™: *Quick & Easy Ways to Make Your Life Fun, Exciting & Vibrant* by Maryann V. Troiani & Michael W. Mercer
Price: $20
❑ Check here if you want Maryann & Michael to autograph book to you

_____ *Turning Your Human Resources Department into a Profit Center*™ by Michael W. Mercer
Price: $65
❑ Check here if you want Michael to autograph to you

253

Audiobooks

Print quantity you want on line provided.

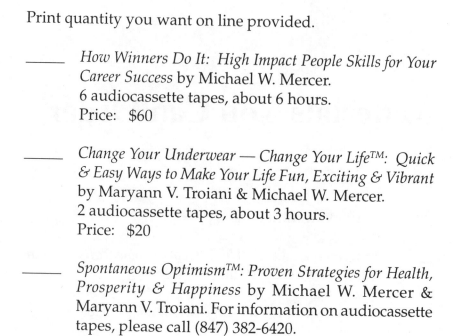

_____   *How Winners Do It: High Impact People Skills for Your Career Success* by Michael W. Mercer.
6 audiocassette tapes, about 6 hours.
Price: $60

_____   *Change Your Underwear — Change Your Life*™: *Quick & Easy Ways to Make Your Life Fun, Exciting & Vibrant* by Maryann V. Troiani & Michael W. Mercer.
2 audiocassette tapes, about 3 hours.
Price: $20

_____   *Spontaneous Optimism*™: *Proven Strategies for Health, Prosperity & Happiness* by Michael W. Mercer & Maryann V. Troiani. For information on audiocassette tapes, please call (847) 382-6420.

Speeches & Workshops

Michael and Maryann can deliver customized speeches and workshops at your organization or conference. For information, call (847) 382-6420.

Intensive Coaching^{SM} Sessions

To schedule an Intensive Coaching™ session conducted by Dr. Troiani or Dr. Mercer, call (847) 382-6420.

Tests

(1-time offer per person or company)

❑ *Behavior Forecaster*™ test to predict 3 interpersonal skills, 5 personality traits, and 5 motivations.
Price: $15

❑ *Abilities Forecaster*™ tests to assess 5 of your mental abilities, namely, your abilities in problem-solving, vocabulary, arithmetic, grammar, and handling small details.
Price: $15

Full-Spectrum Lights

For full-spectrum light bulbs and light boxes, call (847) 382-6420.

All book, audiobook and test prices include shipping & handling in U.S.A. and Canada. Add U.S. $20 for shipping to other nations.

Order by mail, phone, or fax from:

CASTLEGATE PUBLISHERS, INC.
830 West Main Street, Suite 107
Lake Zurich, Illinois, U.S.A. 60047
Phone = (847) 382-6420
Fax = (847) 382-2250

About the Authors

Michael W. Mercer, Ph.D., and Maryann V. Troiani, Psy.D., are psychologists and co-authors. Drs. Mercer and Troiani developed the groundbreaking Intensive Coaching^SM method geared to helping people develop optimistic lives. They have appeared as guests on over 500 radio and TV talk shows, including multiple appearances on *The Oprah Winfrey Show*. Each year, they deliver over 100 speeches and workshops in the U.S., Canada, and Europe. Major magazines and newspapers frequently quote them.

Dr. Mercer is an industrial psychologist, specializing in helping corporations and managers. He authored three business and professional books: (1) *How Winners Do It: High Impact People Skills for Your Career Success*, (2) *Turning Your Human Resources Department into a Profit Center*™, and (3) *Hire the Best — & Avoid the Rest*™. Dr. Mercer also developed two pre-employment tests — the *Behavior Forecaster*™ test and the *Abilities Forecaster*™ test — that many companies use to help choose productive, dependable job applicants.

Dr. Troiani is a clinical psychologist, specializing in helping individuals and groups. She held many leadership positions in the mental health field, including (1) mental health director of an insurance company, (2) director of an eating disorders treatment program, and (3) director of a women's treatment program. She conducts Intensive Coaching^SM sessions with people across the U.S.